D1558818

7 RULES FOR THE PERFECT PUPPY

Everything You Need to Know About Training, Raising, and Caring for Your New Dog in One Book!

RICHARD MELTON

CONTENTS

INTRODUCTION

You've just acquired a new puppy. What an exciting time!

Like toddlers, they must learn to respect boundaries. They can't stop themselves from acting like puppies. You are responsible for showing them how to be a dog.

However, your puppy is well worth it. Dogs are highly beneficial! The journey entails much more than merely having a buddy. Dogs have so much to teach us. They:

- love unconditionally
- live in the moment
- never carry grudges, and
- are never vindictive

Besides, bringing a puppy into your home comes with its own set of obstacles. You'll have to teach your new pet many things in order for you and your pup to get along. Training your puppy will aid in the development of a satisfying bond.

Don't worry, though: you're in good hands!

This puppy training handbook is ideal for you. You'll learn all the necessary things you need to know to train your puppy to be a well-behaved dog!

No fluff

Each chapter of **7 Rules for the Perfect Puppy** is reasonably practical, and we're not wasting any time.

There's a lot to teach your new best buddy, and while puppy training may seem daunting at first, the good news is that you've got an eager student on the other end of the leash. Puppies are eager to learn excellent manners as soon as you bring them home, so now is the best time to begin puppy obedience training.

All animals, including puppies, learn from their moms. When you bring your puppy home, though, it's up to you to be their leader and teach them everything they need to know to grow up to be well-rounded adult canines!

As puppy owners, we all dream of having the perfect puppy - a puppy leisurely strolling behind you or quietly sitting at your feet at an outdoor café. However, there are some things to do to ensure your puppy is on the right track with their training.

A puppy may bring much happiness into your life. However, obedience training is an important aspect of socializing dogs. If you do not provide proper training, your dog will find it difficult to integrate with your family, friends, and other canines.

This might be difficult or embarrassing in some instances. And it could have disastrous repercussions in extreme circumstances.

As a responsible dog owner, it is your job to ensure that your dog is properly trained. You should teach your dog obedience when it's still a puppy. Your dog will be much more open to instruction and have a better potential for learning throughout this period of its life.

Obedience lessons are also an excellent way for your dog to gain socialization with other dogs. We provide all of the reasons why training your dog is crucial and simple methods for doing so in this book.

Below are some of the things we will discuss:

- Understanding your pup's body language and getting inside his head

- How to teach your dog the top five commands: "Sit," "Stay," "Lie Down," "Recall," and "Heel."

- Why should you crate-train your dog?

- How to deal with bad habits like biting, jumping, and barking excessively.

- Housebreaking

- Plus, there is a slew of additional helpful hints and ideas for parenting your puppy!

Everything from how you greet your puppy (are you allowing them to jump up on your legs?), to how you walk them on a leash (are you following as they drag you along?) will teach your dog what conduct is and isn't acceptable.

Even if the training you give your puppy when you initially bring them home appears simple, it will provide the framework for "higher learning" as they grow older. Remember that training is never complete, and success is contingent on the daily performance of new behaviors in new settings!

Nipping, potty accidents, chewing, barking, and other issues will arise as the puppy matures. Your puppy is fast growing. Your puppy should be comfortable with the elements of a daily routine after a few weeks at home, and you should be working on obedience training and learning basic commands.

So, how do you know where to start with your puppy's training? No matter how young your new puppy is when you bring them home, you can use this book as a guide to help your pup grow, develop, and learn the good behaviors they need in their new home and in the world, allowing you to mold them into the wonderful dog you imagined!

A well-behaved puppy is a joy to have around. Let's figure out how to make it happen. I hope you're looking forward to it! Let's get this party started.

CHAPTER ONE

RULE 1: TRUST IS THE MOST IMPORTANT THING!

Today is the most wonderful day of the year! Not Christmas, New Year's Eve, or even your birthday, though they might coincide. Finally, it's time to bring your new puppy home!

You chose the puppy and conducted extensive research. You bought new toys and a collar with his name spelled out in gleaming new letters. You've scheduled an appointment with the veterinarian and determined the ideal spot for him to play. Everything is in place for your new furry companion to move in!

This may be a time of anticipation and planning for you, but to a puppy, it's all new. So while the experience is thrilling, it can also be frightening. Have no fear! There are several things you may do to assist your puppy in acclimating to his new life and smooth the transition.

This chapter will teach you about the importance of developing a trusting relationship between a puppy and his owner. You'll also learn how to adjust the puppy to changes in his environment, how a puppy thinks at different stages of growth, and when to begin training him.

The first week you and your new puppy spend together will be exciting, but it will also be unsettling.

Moving to a new house with a new family is stressful for pups, and it can be stressful for you as well. By planning ahead of time, you can make the adjustment simpler for both of you.

Here are some things to consider before bringing your new puppy home, as well as some initial actions to take once he has joined your family.

BEFORE YOUR NEW PUPPY COMES HOME

You'll need to prepare even before your new puppy arrives at your house. These measures will help your pup get off to the greatest possible start in his new life.

1. Hold a family gathering

A puppy is a big commitment, so ensure everyone in your family is on board with wanting one before you take the plunge.

Then pick who will be the primary caregiver; otherwise, you'll spend lots of time arguing as your new puppy stares at their empty food bowl.

Establish house rules ahead of time to prevent confusing the puppy – will the dog be permitted on the bed? On the sofa? Where is the dog going to sleep? Are there areas of the house that are off-limits? To guarantee that everyone is on the same page, involve the entire family in the decision-making process.

2. Purchase supplies

Purchase some necessities ahead of time so that you and your dog can settle in without having to go to the store frequently.

To get started, you'll need the following:

- A crate
- Food and possibly treats for training – consult your veterinarian about a suitable diet.
- Bowls for food and water
- Collar and leash
- Toys, especially chew toys
- A dog bed
- Cleaners that remove stains and odors

- Perhaps baby or dog gates to block off some areas of your home

3. Get your home ready

If you're acquiring a puppy, you'll have to put in a little extra work. Some puppies are champion chewers and get into things they shouldn't. However, regardless of your dog's age, you should plan ahead of time.

Create a temporary, gated living room for your dog or puppy where they won't be able to trash your belongings or ingest anything toxic. When you're not around, they'll stay in this area to avoid having housetraining accidents.

To ensure your dog doesn't feel alone, choose a room in your house that is a center of activity and has easy-to-clean floors. The kitchen is a popular choice; if necessary, you can close it off with baby gates. Remove anything you don't want chewed or dirty from the equation.

What's in your dog's area depends on their age and how you're housetraining them.

Keep medications, poisons, and certain plants out of reach of your puppy by dog-proofing the space.

4. Make home care arrangements

You should take a few days to a week off work to settle in with your new puppy or dog and begin housetraining. This will also help the two of you bond which will make training easier.

Even if you can take some time off, you'll need to put together a backup team immediately. Look around your neighborhood for dog walkers, pet sitters, or doggie daycare. Rely on word-of-mouth referrals from friends and relatives.

5. Locate an excellent trainer or class

Group obedience sessions are excellent for connecting with your new dog as well as learning how to communicate and train them. These lessons are particularly beneficial to young puppies since they allow them to get more comfortable with other dogs and people, which is vital for developing a safe, friendly dog.

You'll want to carry out some research to ensure you've chosen the right program and instructor because dog training is un-regulated and anyone can call themselves a dog trainer.

6. Plan your return journey

Bring a friend or relative with you to pick up your puppy. Young puppies who have never been in a car before may become nervous. Even mature dogs can get frightened, and a terrifying car ride might turn into a lifelong fear of driving.

On the way home, have someone sit next to your dog to soothe them and keep them from jumping on your lap while you're driving.

You can put your puppy in the crate for the ride home if they are used to it. Just make sure he is secure; sliding around in the backseat will only add to the tension of the journey.

ONCE YOUR PUPPY IS HOME

Getting a new puppy is an enormously gratifying experience, but there will be an adjustment period when bringing any pet home. Like us, dogs enjoy having a schedule, so it's critical to maintain consistency throughout the first several weeks to help your dog acclimate to their new home.

Whether you've just gotten an older dog or a new puppy, you should expect them to take a few days to acclimate, but these recommendations will make the process go more smoothly. Here's how to make your dog more comfortable in your home.

How to Assist Your Pup in Adjusting to Your New Home

These suggestions will assist your new dog in settling into his new home and will strengthen your bond with him. It could take a day or two, or it could take months, depending on the puppy's nature and experiences. It takes time for a puppy to acclimate from a shelter to a home, so don't be discouraged if it takes more time for your puppy to settle in.

Here are 10 suggestions to assist your new puppy in acclimatizing to your home to make the move easier.

1. Start slowly to allow your pup to decompress.

Slowly help your pup acclimatize to your environment. He'll value some one-on-one time learning about his new family and environments. Allow him to take his time walking around the yard and house.

Some puppies take a long time to adjust to new surroundings, which can be exhausting. If you adopted your puppy/dog from a shelter, keep in mind that he presumably comes from a stressful and busy environment, and your comfortable and peaceful home will be the first place he's slept well in a long time.

Don't overstimulate your puppy for the first few days. Allow your puppy to investigate things for himself if he is wary. If he comes to you for attention, be as affectionate as he appears to be comfortable with.

Don't take it personally if your dog doesn't bond with you right away. He's in an unfamiliar setting, adjusting to new sights, smells, and sounds. It might be a stressful time for your new puppy, so try to keep things as calm and positive as possible.

2. Provide your puppy with his own space

One method to make your new puppy feel more at ease in letting him have his own secure space or soft bed where he can retire when he's tired or overwhelmed. Some puppies require a little additional time to relax every now and again, especially given the stress of being in an unfamiliar place.

If your new puppy isn't interested in cuddling or playing, give him something to do on his own, such as a food-dispensing toy or a stuffed Kong. Putting food in a Kong tells your new puppy that you're a terrific provider. It's a simple approach to establishing trust, and if your puppy is nervous in his new environment, he might appreciate a lovely treat alone.

3. Be prepared for stomach issues when switching food

Diarrhea is common in newly adopted puppies, which can be caused by stress or drastic food changes. To avoid an upset stomach from a sudden change in nutrition, ask the shelter or rescue organization what food your dog has been consuming. If you don't like the food they've been eating, you can switch, but you should try transitioning them gradually by mixing part of the old food with the new.

In freshly adopted puppies, stress from adjusting to a new environment can induce diarrhea. Take it slowly the first week to ease their anxiety and give them time to acclimate. Consult your veterinarian if your pup's diarrhea lasts more than a few days.

4. In new environments, dogs may lose their appetite

The pressure of being in a new environment can impact a dog's appetite. It may take some days for a timid puppy to feel comfortable eating a regular meal. A change in food or diet might also cause a dog to refuse to eat. Your dog will not starve to death; as long as he is in good physical shape, he will adjust to his new food.

If you're worried about your puppy's appetite, give them a high-value treat like chicken or ham. If they're willing to eat high-value food, they're probably just getting used to it. If your dog refuses to eat high-value food after a few days, consult your veterinarian.

5. Keep your routine to make it easier in the long run

Dogs excel on routine, and the earlier your new puppy learns how to operate in your home, the more at ease he will be. You may help your new puppy in adapting to your home by:

- Consistently going outside for potty breaks
- Feeding at the same time every day
- Taking your regular walk at the same time
- Getting into bed at the same time every night

This includes any workout, snuggle, or other daily games or activities he will participate in. Once he knows your routine and what is expected of him at any given time, he will feel more secure.

Many owners, I'm sure, want to spend as much time as possible with their new puppy, which is fantastic. However, for the first few weeks, try to mix at least part of your typical activities into the day to assist your dog in acclimatizing to what will eventually become his usual pattern.

6. Supervise your new pet

If your puppy is already crate trained, you may want to try leaving him in it while you work, especially if you have other pets at home. When left alone, some dogs can become destructive or agitated.

Crating is a good way to have peace of mind while at work if you're unsure how your new puppy will react when left alone. Simply remember to slowly introduce your dog to their crate and make it a lovely experience for them. When used appropriately, a crate may become a soothing environment for your dog.

7. You may have a few issues with house training.

House training is required for puppies, but you should also expect some house training challenges with recently adopted dogs.

Be prepared for a few blunders in the first few weeks if you and your newly adopted dog don't have the same routine right away. Your new puppy may eat more regularly and drink more than usual. Make sure you take him out regularly to lessen the risks of an accident.

8. Be mindful of attempts to run away

Remember to keep your new puppy on a leash whenever you go outside. Some dogs will attempt to escape or flee when introduced to a new environment. Also, because dogs can dig under or jump over fences, you should never leave your dog alone in the yard. It's preferable to keep your dog leashed outside until you know he is familiar with you and will return when called.

9. If they're nervous, don't overwhelm them.

It's tempting to bring all of your friends and family over to meet your new puppy immediately, but make sure your dog is comfortable in your home first. This enthusiasm might cause some dogs to become overstimulated and exuberant, while others become quite fearful around strangers. If your dog appears to be in discomfort, take it slowly. Ascertain that they have their safe zone or area to retreat if they become overwhelmed.

The same goes for trips to the store or park. Take it slow while introducing your dog to new places until they are comfortable with you.

10. Show your new dog patience

Consider yourself in your puppy's shoes (or paws) in an unknown area surrounded by strangers. It's terrifying. Your dog could take days or weeks to acclimate. Each dog is an individual with his own story to tell. Some puppies come from a loving family and may adapt more easily, while others have been waiting for years at a shelter.

Slow down and make things easy for them by giving them room when they need it. Give them enough time to familiarize themselves with their new surroundings and settle in. Although it may be a lengthy process, your adopted dog will quickly become your new best buddy.

STAGES OF PUPPY DEVELOPMENT AND BEHAVIOR

You must meet your dog's demands at each stage of development if you want him to be well-adjusted and social. Building a fantastic dog starts with adequate training at each stage of development and establishing appropriate guidelines to ensure that your puppy is adequately integrated into the family.

Throughout your puppy's life, you will notice numerous behavioral changes. Knowing how to care for your puppy at each stage of development can help you mold him into a lifetime family member.

Stages of Puppy Development

There are five stages to the puppy development process. Puppies, however, progress through these stages at their own rate; therefore, timetables may vary.

First stage: Neonatal Period (0–2 weeks)

Starting at birth, this is the first stage of puppy development. Puppies have just the senses of taste and touch at this age and rely entirely on their mother.

Second stage: Transitional Period (2–4 weeks)

Hearing and smell are two more senses that continue to grow. Puppy teeth begin to emerge, and their eyes open. This is also when your puppy's personality starts to emerge. Puppies play with each other, wag their tails, stand, walk a short distance, and bark.

Third stage: Socialization Period (3 – 12 weeks)

This is the most crucial period in the growth of a puppy. It's critical to understand this stage because most puppies are adopted between 7 and 12 weeks of age. Changes occur quickly during this time.

Puppies start to become aware of their environment and have the ability to form relationships with people when they are between 3-5 weeks old. This is the time when puppies become accustomed to the sounds of everyday life, such as televisions, vacuum cleaners, and telephones.

Puppies are just learning to interact and play at this age. They're also honing their canine social skills and figuring out where they fit in their pack's hierarchy. Their biting skills are improving, as is their interest. Biting habits develop as they practice biting with their mother and littermates.

They have full command of all of their senses at 7-9 weeks of age and are ready to go home to their new parents.

Your puppy's socialization stage begins when you bring him home (typically between 7 and 12 weeks of age). As a result, it's critical that you expose your puppy to as many new dogs, people, things, and environments as possible. However, make sure you do so in a controlled manner and never place your puppy in a dangerous environment where they could be hurt, scared, or infected.

For many reasons, now is the perfect time to start crate training. Puppies are old enough to get used to being left alone in order to avoid separation anxiety and they are capable of housetraining. Your home is undoubtedly puppy proof, but it also protects your belongings.

Puppies develop their reactions to objects much more reliably at this stage of development. They are also likely to pay attention to a variety of people and be pleasant and approachable to strangers. They will also continue to improve their biting skills throughout this period! It is vital to understand how to regulate this behavior as soon as possible.

You may also discover that they are more curious and will want to learn more about their surroundings. Prepare for this by keeping your puppy leashed and near to you.

Fourth stage: Testing Period (3 – 6 months)

This is when your puppy begins to push the boundaries of their environment. They will test the limits of their owners and other animals. At this age, many older dogs will start to enforce manners. Throughout this time, problematic behaviors may emerge. Make sure you start a training program with your dog if you haven't previously. Finding a solid positive training class is fantastic, but you must also practice at home on a regular (daily) basis.

Your puppy will be teething at this age, and chewing will be a common side effect. Before your puppy begins to chew on your furniture, make the following adjustments:

- Do not leave him alone unattended.

- Provide him with a variety of chew sticks and toys.

- Use commercial sprays or gels to keep your dog from chewing on your personal items.

If your puppy is in agony due to teething, try soaking a cloth toy in chicken stock and freezing it. This can be given to your puppy as a chew toy to help soothe sore gums. When the upper fangs (canines) come in at six months, puppies are usually done teething.

Fifth stage: Adolescence (6–18 months).

Adolescence might be the most challenging stage of a puppy's growth. Your adorable puppy is approaching puberty and will begin to produce hormones, which may cause behavioral changes. Adolescence begins significantly earlier in dogs than in humans; for small breeds, it can start as early as months, while larger dogs start at nine or ten months. Larger breed dogs go through adolescence until they are two or three years old, while smaller dogs mature at around 18 months. The slower the development, the larger the dog is.

Puberty Symptoms in Dogs

The following are some of the common symptoms that your dog has reached puberty:

Males:

- Testicular degeneration

- Scent marking

- Marking with his leg raised (pee)

- Loss of friendliness

- Increased interest in roaming, decreased interest in following orders

- Lifting his leg indoors.

- Hostility among male dogs.

Females:

- It usually begins with the first heat cycle.

- Displays of unpredictable behavior

- Moodiness

- Displays of hostility

- Lethargy

Some or all of the above signs may or may not be visible. As your puppy matures, most of these behaviors will fade away if you continue to train and socialize him during this time.

Giving an adolescent dog plenty of daily exercise and continuing positive training sessions on a regular basis is one of the best strategies to help him get through this stage. Routine and consistency are essential. Please see your veterinarian, dog behaviorist, or trained trainer if your dog begins to exhibit aggressive behavior.

Periods of Fear

Puppies go through four fear phases on average during their growth. These are around the following ages:

- From 8 to 10 weeks

- From 4 to 6 months

- Approximately 9 months

- Between the ages of 14 - 18 months

This is a critical stage in a puppy's growth and can lead to hostility if managed incorrectly. When your puppy enters a fear period, he becomes terrified of something he previously ignored or was unconcerned with. Hunching down, shivering, backing away, hiding, running away, or submissively urinating could be his reaction. Growling, barking, raising his hackles, or exposing fangs are all examples of more pronounced behaviors.

In any case, whenever you notice any of these behaviors in your puppy, you should stop taking them to new places and introducing them to new things for about a week. If at all possible, avoid scheduling any veterinarian appointments during this time.

Rough Play, Biting, and Nipping

When beginning puppy training, make sure to include some instruction that biting, mouthing, chewing, and rough play are all inappropriate behaviors.... for us. These are, however, natural puppy behaviors, and punishment will not work. Redirection is crucial.

Inhibition is a puppy behavior in which the animal learns to control the intensity of its behaviors (bites, rough play, etc.). It's a vital part of pet socialization since it's how puppies learn how much is acceptable and how much is excessive. Puppies learn that biting too forcefully hurts their siblings or mother and puts an end to play. They quickly modify their biting strength to a milder bite and resume play. This also occurs during rough play.

Invest in proper chew toys that you can direct your puppy toward to keep yourself and your family from becoming chew toys.

BITING

Providing feedback on the appropriate amount of force they can use when biting or playing can also benefit them (and ultimately you). The following guidelines are for biting, although they can also be used for rough play.

Before they reach maturity, puppies must learn to bite lightly for their own and your sake. Adult dogs constantly play with each other using their lips. A puppy who hasn't acquired biting inhibition risks injuring other canines or humans.

Say "OUCH" very loud and leave the room for 1-2 minutes the first time your puppy bites. By doing so, you're simulating the reaction other puppies might have if a puppy bit them too hard. He'll be left alone.

When you get back, keep playing until he bites you again. Repeat the procedure if he bites you again. You may be required to repeat the process several times, but your dog should finally pick it up. This should be done with your puppy by several persons, excluding minors.

A tiny percentage of puppies will become thrilled by any verbal response to their biting, which will cause them to bite harder. If your puppy exhibits this behavior, remain silent and leave the area for 1-2 minutes. Excessive mouthing in pups is often an indication of exhaustion, and a nap in a crate, x-pen, or quiet room can help.

Understanding each stage of puppy development will help you anticipate what to expect in terms of growth and behavior. You'll also be better prepared to give your puppy the proper care at each stage, lowering the chances of your puppy ending up in a shelter.

Finally, you are more likely to produce a well-balanced, emotionally secure, and safe dog if you provide a consistent routine, consistency, good training, and enough socialization and exercise.

HOW DO I GET MY DOG TO TRUST ME?

As their caregivers, we are honored to have our canine companions' trust. But what if your dog has had a traumatic encounter that leaves them distrustful of humans? Is there anything you can do to gain their trust because they feel safe, confident, and loved? Absolutely. You can begin to break through the barriers your dog has erected with a little time and patience.

The Effects of Trust on a Dog's Mental Health

Dogs who appear to trust you do so because they are neither afraid nor uneasy in your presence or in their surroundings. Making your dog feel comfortable is key to building trust. A dog's trust in you gives them the assurance that contact with you will result in positive outcomes. As a result of this, not only will the number of interactions rise, but trusting canines will actively seek out chances to interact with persons they trust. Your dog will get more confidence as a result of this.

A dog who is worried and scared, on the other hand, will appear not to trust you and may avoid affectionate gestures such as patting, refuse to engage in play and other pleasant activities, and lack excitement when welcoming their human companion when they return home at the end of the day. Anxious and fearful dogs may hide from you or others and show little interest in interacting. If you force these dogs to interact with you, they may snarl, bark, nip at you, or try to bite you, therefore it's critical to read your dog's behavior rather than forcing them into activities.

How to Earn Your Dog's Trust

Building trust takes time and patience, but there are some things you can do to help your dog feel more at ease and trust you. Some of the following techniques should help you get started, depending on your dog's individual condition and how they demonstrate their trust.

Recognize their body language.

A happy and content puppy will have a relaxed face and body, wag his tail back and forth, and hold his tail high. A nervous or anxious dog will have a rigid body, keep his tail low or tucked under their body, avoid eye contact, pant, or pace.

Look for other indicators of worry and fear.

Cowering, low or flat ears, standing still and stiff or moving slowly, a curling lip, snarling, raised hackles, shaking, turning away, whimpering, yawning, or lip licking are examples of these behaviors. Schedule an appointment with your vet for evaluation and advice if your dog exhibits signs of severe fear and anxiety (such as snarling, nipping, biting, a frozen or stiff stance, or running away).

Allow your dog to set the pace.

Maintain a comfortable pace for your dog. Rushing or pushing beyond his limits will stifle improvement.

Please respect your dog's personal space.

You might wish to lavish your dog with unconditional love. However, shy and skittish dogs might not be ready for this. Allow time to pass, walk slowly, avoid your gaze, and speak quietly.

Get down to the dog's level.

It's crucial to get down to their level since towering over dogs might make them afraid and uncomfortable. Squat down or sit on the floor so that you are at eye level with them. Maintain a safe distance from the dog and ignore them until they approach you.

Allow your dog to approach you.

When your dog approaches, greet him with a happy, calm voice and a tasty treat. Take note of your puppy's reaction to the treat. If he takes it from you harshly and/or drops the treat, it's a sign that he's nervous and afraid. Instead of touching the dog, speak softly to him and provide a few more treats. Then give him space. You may proceed if they gently take the treat from you and eat it right away, pet them if they allow it by lightly stroking their chest or chin with your hand extended from underneath. This underhanded method is critical because a hand elevated above a dog's head can be frightening to them.

Observe your dog while you touch them and use the "consent test" to assess if the interaction is comfortable for him. Count to three while caressing him. Then check whether he leans in for further petting or shows you that he is enjoying the attention in some other way. Allow him to stop the interaction with verbal praise if they choose to move away, snarl, adopt a stiff stance, or show any of the indicators of fear and anxiety listed above. Allow him his personal space. This builds trust by demonstrating to your dog that you "listen" to his body language and don't touch him if he doesn't want to be touched.

CHAPTER TWO

RULE 2: GET PUPPIES USED TO A POTTY AT A CERTAIN TIME AND PLACE

Whether you call it housebreaking, housetraining, or potty training, all new dog owners want to teach their new puppy not to mess in their new home. The most effective strategy to attain this goal is to create and stick to a timeline.

While you're sticking to your schedule, it's a good idea to clearly define the rules for where your puppy can and shouldn't go potty, and dog crates and puppy pads can be beneficial training tools in this regard.

This chapter explains how to train a puppy to use the potty, including a daily schedule and a message that the puppy must be accustomed to at a specific time and location.

One of the most crucial things you can do with your new puppy is house training (or potty training). Everyone is happy when the puppy understands where and when to go potty. When potty training a puppy, keep in mind that it's natural for a puppy to see the entire world as one big potty area. Regular outings, competent management, adequate supervision, and positive reinforcement are the keys to teaching your dog where to go potty. (Potty training doesn't allow punishment!) It will take time and care, but you and your dog can accomplish this vital task.

So, how long does potty training a dog take? That is mainly determined by your consistency and how long your puppy can hold it. (For example, small breed puppies have more difficulty holding it than large breed puppies.) The stages for potty training a puppy in seven days are listed below—you may discover that it takes a bit longer with your puppy, which is fine! But first, how often do puppies need to go outside?

POTTY TRAINING FOR A PUPPY

It's all about setting yourself and your puppy up for success in potty training. Successful house training requires proper administration and supervision. Ensure that your puppy is always controlled or supervised until he or she is entirely house trained.

Follow the outlined steps below to complete this process effectively.

1. Select a Training Technique

Potty training puppies is done in various ways by various pet parents. Pet parents commonly use a dog box or a dog training pad. Each of these tools has distinct advantages at different stages of the training process.

If you want to educate your puppy to utilize training pads, you'll need to determine which type is ideal for his needs and your preferences. Choose pads that fit your dog's size, and give your puppy plenty of time to become used to them before they need to be used. When your pet needs to go potty, gently lead them to the pad and encourage them to go.

Another excellent method for potty training your puppy is to use a crate. Because dogs rarely "go" in the same location they sleep in, crate training is a possible option. After taking your puppy for a nighttime pee break, take them to their crate. When they wake up, take him straight to the bathroom for some morning relief.

Although your puppy may initially reject the idea of a crate, he will ultimately know it as a safe haven. While puppies may occasionally urinate inside the box, necessitating cleanup, crate training is still essential to your puppy's ultimate objective.

2. Establish a Routine

It's critical to stick to a schedule. Your dog will begin to form expectations for the day based on the schedule you create at an early age. When you incorporate training into your everyday routine, your puppy will learn the proper time to go pee.

It doesn't have to be complicated. If you can give your puppy a schedule, they will learn when to wake up, eat, exercise, and sleep. The most crucial thing they'll learn is when to expect breaks throughout the day.

Choose a location

Identifying an area in your yard or home where your dog should "go" makes potty training easier. Lead your dog to the location where they need to go potty and wait. After your dog has become accustomed to one environment, returning to it can make them feel more confident.

Frequently go to the potty spot

Especially at the start of the training process, puppies need to be frequently taken to their pee area. If you're teaching your puppy to go potty outside, for example, getting them used to a daily walk routine will help them learn to contain their bladder in anticipation of a trip outside. Encourage your puppy to use his or her indoor potty whenever they need to relieve themselves.

Regular potty breaks for your dog might also help you avoid accidents. Consider going to the potty spot after your dog wakes up, after meals, drinking plenty of water, and right before bedtime. These trips will help them avoid accidents and allow them to go potty at a location you specify.

Follow a feeding schedule

A puppy's potty trips will usually coincide with their eating schedule. Time how long your puppy needs to go potty after supper because every puppy is different. This will assist you in planning meal times around your puppy's chosen restroom schedule.

Changes in your dog's diet can have an effect on when they need to go potty. If you make any changes to your dog's food or feeding schedule, keep track of how it affects their toilet breaks and frequency.

Keep an eye on their intake

Water intake, like your dog's meal schedule, has an impact on toilet break timings, length, and frequency. Some pups may eagerly drink large amounts of water when they return from a walk outside, only to require a toilet break minutes later. If possible, assist your puppy in pacing their water intake to avoid the detrimental effects of rushed water intake.

Water consumption also corresponds to your dog's potty breaks. Some puppies prefer to drink water while eating, while others like to separate the two activities. Pay close attention to when your dog consumes water and how much water he drinks to schedule potty breaks.

Provide incentives

Your potty-training attempts will be tremendously aided by positive reinforcement. Praise, chew treats, and puppy chew toys are all effective motivators for many puppies. Give your puppy a reward when he goes potty in the correct location, holds his urine until he reaches the outdoors, or completes another milestone in the potty-training process.

Your puppy will immediately identify your approval with their activities and work even harder to get it in the future.

3. Watch over your puppy

Keeping an eye on your puppy during the day is very important for two reasons: Avoiding indoor accidents and developing healthy interactions with other people and objects; puppies require monitoring. Puppies will frequently chew on things and nip people unless carefully taught otherwise.

Even though there's nothing wrong with giving your puppy some independence, make sure you're always aware of how full his bladder is. Throughout the day, your puppy will communicate with you in various ways, and it is up to you to notice and interpret those signals.

One of the reasons your dog goes potty in the incorrect place could be that you're not paying attention to the indications they give you.

Below are all signs that your puppy has to eliminate:

- Crying, barking, or whining
- Pacing or walking in circles
- Sitting by the door
- Scratching at the door
- Sitting patiently in front of you
- Trembling or shaking

These and other warning signals could appear minutes before an accident, so pay great attention to your dog's body language and behavior when overseeing them.

4. Be prepared for mishaps

While potty training your puppy, you will have accidents. Even if your training goes well, your puppy will most likely have accidents while learning your expectations for them. When your puppy has an accident, your reaction might significantly impact their future behavior.

Avoid yelling or raising your voice when speaking to your puppy, as tempting as it may seem. Aggressive touch with your puppy can be even more harmful because your puppy may develop fear for the potty-training process—or even you.

After your dog urinates in the house, respond amiably but forcefully to prevent indoor mishaps. Even if your dog appears to be done, take them to their potty spot to finish. This will aid in improving their connection to the outdoors and relief.

5. Clean thoroughly

If your dog does urinate on the floor, it's critical that you wipe it up thoroughly. Cleaning up after your dog may seem tedious, but it will help you disinfect your home and keep germs at bay.

Fortunately, some helpful dog cleanup tools make the job simple. Potty training spray, for example, can help you teach your puppy to "go" on a pee pad, tray, or another designated area.

Use an odor-destroying cleaning product on any stains before they become permanent.

6. Seek assistance

Potty training a dog is a challenging and time-consuming chore. It's a fun procedure that helps you bond with your dog, but it can also be stressful. Don't be afraid to ask if you need assistance during the puppy toilet training process.

For best outcomes, keep your approach consistent when potty training your puppy. Keep an eye on your puppy when you can, even if that means asking someone else to look after him while you're gone. If you must leave your puppy alone for more than a few hours, find someone who will give your puppy the same number of breaks as you.

HOW OFTEN DO DOGS NEED TO GO OUTSIDE?

In general, a dog can wait between peeing and pooping for:

- 1 to 2 hours for young pups

- 3 to 4 hours for older puppies who are used to going outdoors to pee and poop

- 8 to 10 hours for adult dogs who are fully housetrained and used to being home alone while you're at work

Little puppies do not understand that they are meant to "hold it" inside the home and only pee and defecate outside. You'll have to teach them from the ground up.

How?

By assuming their thoughts and guessing when they would need to pee or poop. (You'll have to do this until your dog can "tell you" he needs to go outside.)

A 3-MONTH-OLD PUPPY SAMPLE SCHEDULE

Consider that a 3-month-old puppy's urine may be held for up to 4 hours. Schedule potty breaks every four hours into your housetraining program in such a scenario.

You should have a strategy in place and stick to it. Potty training will be a positive experience for your dog if you do this and give him lots of praise.

It is critical to take the puppy outside first thing in the morning. You risk accidents if you wait. Potty time should be held in the same location so that your dog learns to link it with bathroom breaks.

You are advised to also keep your dog on a leash. This way, they won't run in the opposite direction and get hurt. A special command is also recommended by some dog trainers. The late, great Barbara Woodhouse, for example, popularized the phrase "Hurry up" as a verbal cue. Others have used words such as "Make" or even "Poopies."

Using your puppy's sense of smell is one technique to urge him to use the same location every time. To show them where to go, use a small piece of newspaper or a cloth scented with urine.

Bathroom breaks should be taken frequently. Let's assume you had a successful mission at 7 a.m. and wonder when you should take your next potty break. 11 a.m. would be the latest for a 3-month-old puppy. You'll want to go out more regularly if you're just starting with potty training. You may find that every hour or two is best in the first few weeks.

Every three hours is appropriate after your puppy has been accustomed to pee breaks. 7 am., 11 am., 3 pm., 7 p.m., and 11 pm., for example, are ideal times. That doesn't imply your puppy will be able to hold it all night.

A puppy that is three months old will most likely not be able to sleep through the night without going outside. Setting the alarm for 3 a.m. may be the only way to keep the puppy from soiling the house during the night. Fortunately, this time of puppyhood is brief.

After each meal, your dog should also go out for 10 to 15 minutes. The gastrocolic reflex is stimulated by eating, so they'll feel the need to go shortly thereafter. It's important to note that different puppies will need to go to the bathroom at somewhat different times after eating.

When your dog switches from one activity to another, you should take him outside. A critical time is after a nap or after playtime, for example. So, if you're playing games with your dog indoors, you should take him outside afterward. Then you can confidently return him to his crate or playpen.

SITUATIONS FOR PUPPY POTTY TRAINING

1. What to Do If Your Puppy Completes a Successful "Bathroom Run."

"Yay!" Exuberantly praise your puppy. When puppies sense that you are pleased with them, they reply with wagging tails and squirming butts. Make potty training an enjoyable experience for your pet.

The greatest moment to praise your puppy is when they go potty in the appropriate location. Also, don't be afraid to express your joy. Clap your hands, bounce up and down, sing to your dog, whatever it takes to make it feel good for him.

You can also praise your faithful puppy by petting them and giving them a morsel of yummy food. This is one of the greatest forms of positive reinforcement for a job well done.

2. What Should You Do If Your Puppy's "Bathroom Run" Fails

Confinement is the only option if a trip outside proves to be a waste of time. This is especially critical if you know you haven't gone outside in two or three hours. There are four things you may do to assist your puppy in getting back on track.

- Place the puppy in his crate.

- Keep your puppy confined to the kitchen or the laundry area.

- Place the dog in a crate.

- Finally, "umbilical cord training" is available. This is where you attach the puppy to you with a lead. It can be fastened to a belt loop. The puppy can't get away from you this way, and it's easy to keep an eye on them.

This type of confinement should last approximately 15 minutes. The puppy is then taken outside for a second potty break.

It also aids in potty training by maintaining a consistent puppy feeding schedule.

3. What to Do If Your Puppy Pees on the Floor

Accidents occur. Please don't penalize your puppy for urinating inside the house. Dog trainers will tell you that having a puppy means you must constantly monitor them. Then you'll learn to recognize the subtle indicators that your puppy needs to go potty. Circling and sniffing the ground, for example, are traditional signals.

Before they pee inside, you'll be able to take them outdoors. If you can't react quickly enough, try making a loud noise to distract the puppy. This will produce a muscular contraction, allowing you to take the puppy outside and the appropriate location.

The dog should then be praised when he goes potty in the correct location. You can clean the area inside using an odor neutralizer to deal with the stench.

Then take note of the time and make sure you're back on track.

4. What Should You Do If You Must Leave Your Puppy for Longer Than They Can Hold Urine?

This is difficult. If you leave a puppy for longer than they can retain their urine, they will most likely pee. You'll be disappointed, the puppy will be agitated, and your housebreaking routine will be disrupted.

Is it okay if you bring the puppy? If not, do you have a trusted individual who can assist you with potty training and maintaining a consistent schedule?

If you must leave the house for more than 2 or 3 hours, keep the puppy in a small space. You're building a "home" for them by restricting them to a crate or a gated area, and puppies don't want to soil their house. Anything longer than 2 to 3 hours is risky. Furthermore, puppies who are constantly forced to hold their urine beyond their comfort level are at risk. This can lead to a painful urinary tract infection that requires antibiotics.

Pee pads are useful for some new puppy parents when toilet training their puppies. You're teaching your dog to go to a particular spot with pee pads. You set them in a convenient location for your dog and treat them as a potty-training area.

To train your puppy, you'll need to offer a lot of praise. If you live in a high-rise building, pee pads can come in handy. They're particularly helpful if your area has severe weather and it's not always safe to go outside.

CHAPTER THREE

RULE 3: A CRATE IS A COMFORTABLE AND SAFE PLACE FOR A DOG

We all want a well-behaved dog who doesn't destroy things and relieves himself outside, and crate training is a crucial part of that. A crate provides a safe environment for your dog, as well as a personal space.

While many people associate crates with being "confined," dogs are naturally denning animals who prefer to stay in enclosed, compact spaces. Crates give them a sense of safety, and when they're taught to use them from a young age, they can help soothe anxiousness.

You typically go to your couch or bedroom to decompress when you're upset, and a dog's crate provides a similar purpose for puppies. When dogs need to relax or snooze, they can use the crate as a safe place to go.

Because it will quickly become a valued haven for your dog, picking the right crate for his specific needs is critical. Let's look at what to look for while selecting the ideal crate for your dog. But first, why is crate training important?

WHY IS CRATE TRAINING IMPORTANT?

Some years ago, I got my first dog. We always had dogs when I was younger, but this was my first purebred after I moved out of my parents' house. She was a golden retriever from a reputable breeder and proved to be educational for me.

Crates always seemed cruel to me. With the new puppy, I learned that crates are not bad when used correctly and can be a valuable tool for the typical pet owner. Both you and your puppy can benefit from proper, constructive crate training.

Here are my top seven reasons for crate training your dog:

1. Provide a Secure Environment

Crates can provide a safe sanctuary for your dog when he is agitated or exhausted and requires some quiet. When your dog is in his crate, whether by his choice or by yours, children must be educated that he is out of bounds for them and must be left alone.

2. Assistance with House Training

Crates are excellent for housebreaking. Because dogs and puppies dislike a soiled bed, a correctly sized crate can help you teach him bladder and feces control.

3. Domestic Safety

It's a plus to have your dog napping nicely in his crate while you're not there to oversee him. Perhaps you're preparing supper or renovating, and your dog is causing a hazard just by being underfoot. You'll have rest of mind knowing he's safely tucked away.

4. More Secure Travel

It is considerably safer for both of you to have your dog travel in a crate than to have him loose in the car.

5. More Convenient Vet Visits

If your dog has already been crate trained, he will be significantly less stressed if he is confined in the cage or run overnight at the veterinarian.

6. Limitation of Damage

Have you seen those internet "dog shaming" videos where the pet parent returns home to find his furnishings in shambles? Those mishaps may have been averted if the dog had been left in his crate with a bone or toy to gnaw on rather than trashing the designer couch.

7. Emergency Evacuation

Finally, having a crate-trained dog makes it much easier for everyone involved if you ever have to leave your home in a crisis or emergency. Whether you keep your puppy with you or have to leave him with others, he will be happier in his crate. He'll be more relaxed if he has his own blankets and toys with your scent on them, rather than an unfamiliar crate that is stressful for him.

WHAT ARE THE THINGS TO LOOK FOR IN A DOG CRATE

It's difficult for a new pet parent to know what to look for when selecting an ideal crate. To assist you, we've broken down the various materials, the size of a dog crate that should be used, and the optimal size for your dog.

When to use each of the four crate types

You'll come across four typical crate kinds when shopping for your pet's crate: wire, plastic, soft-sided, and wooden dog crates.

1. Wire crates are easily transportable and storable. For pets with long coats or those who live in hotter areas, this sort of enclosure allows plenty of airflow.

2. Plastic crates are made of a strong and long-lasting substance. This is great for families who frequently travel with some who must meet airline restrictions.

3. Soft-sided crates are ideal for small breed dogs or pups who are used to being confined. This confinement is simple to set up and takedown thanks to the lightweight and flexible materials.

4. Style-conscious families will appreciate wooden crates. They come in a number of styles that you may be able to integrate in your home decor for a long-term containment solution.

What size crate will be comfortable for my dog?

You may now have a better notion of what sort of crate is best for your dog, but you may still be unsure of what size crate to buy. Crates are available in several sizes to accommodate dogs of various shapes and sizes. Choose a dog crate that allows your dog to stand up, turn around, stretch out, and lie down when determining how big it should be. Any extra space will encourage your pet to sleep on one side of the box while disregarding the other.

Many crates come with recommended weight ranges, but you should consider your dog's physical attributes and weight. Although a long-legged Whippet and a chubby, short-legged Pembroke Welsh Corgi may weigh the same, the two breeds will have distinct requirements when it comes to selecting a suitable crate in which to sleep. Consider the height and length of the crates while you shop to choose one that is the most comfortable for your pet.

We recommend following the steps below to establish the optimal measurements for the crate you purchase in order to best determine the size crate your dog will require. After you've measured your dog, check the product specifications to discover which size is ideal for you.

- Measure your dog's length from the tip of his snout to the base of his tail while he is standing.

- Measure your dog's height from the top of his head to the ground while sitting.

- Add 4 inches to your dog's length and height measurements and use those values to shop for the proper crate dimensions.

When getting a puppy, bear in mind that he will grow! Expect to buy a larger crate as they develop, or estimate the proper crate size based on their projected adult size and search for a divider that can expand with your pup.

Consider the future while choosing a crate for your puppy. Choose a crate that your pet can grow into rather than one that fits their current size. If you choose this route, make sure the crate you buy has moveable crate dividers so you can adjust the amount of space for your puppy as he grows. You can also reduce the size of the crate by placing a cardboard box on one side of it until your pet outgrows it (however, if your puppy is a chewer, this may not be a good option for them).

THE CRATE TRAINING PROCESS

Crate training can take days or weeks, depending on your dog's age. When crate training, keep two things in mind: the crate should always be associated with something nice, and training should be done in small steps. Don't go too fast.

Step 1: Teach your puppy how to use the crate.

Place the container in a family room or other section of the house where the family spends a lot of time. Place a comfortable blanket or a bed in the crate. Remove the door or prop it open to let the dog explore the crate at their leisure. Some dogs are naturally intrigued and will immediately begin napping in the crate.

- Bring them over to the box and talk to them in a pleasant tone of voice. Ensure the crate door is open and securely fastened to avoid hitting or frightening your dog.

- Place small treats near the crate door, then just inside the door, and then all the way inside to entice your dog to enter. If your puppy refuses to go all the way in at first, it's okay; don't push him.

- Continue to throw goodies into the crate until your dog walks quietly inside the crate to retrieve the food. If treats aren't appealing, try putting a beloved toy in the crate. This phase could take anywhere from a few minutes to several days.

Step 2: Feed your dog in the crate.

After your dog has been introduced to his crate, start serving them their regular meals near it. This will create a pleasant connection with the crate.

- If your dog enters the crate easily when you start Step 2, place the full food dish or interactive puzzle toy at the far back of the crate.

- If he still refuses to enter, only place the dish inside as far as he can go without being frightened or concerned. Each time you feed him, move the dish further back in the crate.

- When your dog is standing comfortably in the crate, close the door while he eats. When you first do this, open the door as soon as he stops eating. Leave the door closed a few minutes longer with each successful feeding until he stays inside the crate for ten minutes or more after eating.

- If they begin whining to be let out, you may have increased the time too quickly. Try to let them stay in the crate for a shorter period of time next time.

Step 3: Try longer crating times.

While you're at home, you can confine your dog in the crate for short periods of time if he has been eating his regular meals there with no signs of anxiety or distress.

- Invite him to the crate and reward him with a treat.

- Use a speech cue to invite him in, such as "crate." With a treat in your hand, point to the interior of the crate to encourage him.

- Praise your dog as he enters the crate, then give him the treat and shut the door.

- Go into a separate room for a few minutes after sitting calmly near the crate for five to ten minutes. Return, sit gently for a few moments, and then release him.

- Repeat this process several times a day, progressively increasing the amount of time the dog spends in the box, as well as the amount of time you're out of sight.

- You can start keeping your dog in the crate when you leave for short periods of time and/or let him sleep there at night once he can stay quietly in the crate for more than 20 minutes with you mostly out of sight. This could take a few days or weeks.

Step 4, Part I: Crate your dog when you go out.

You can start putting your dog in the crate for short amounts of time when you leave the house after they can stay about 30 minutes without becoming anxious or fearful.

- Use your standard command and a treat to place them in the crate. You might also keep a few safe toys in the crate for them to play with.

- Change the time you put your dog in the crate during your "getting ready to leave" routine. Although they shouldn't be crated for an extended period of time before leaving, you can do so anywhere between five and 20 minutes before leaving.

- Don't make your departures emotional or lengthy; they should be brief. Praise your dog briefly before rewarding them with a treat for entering the crate.

When you get home, don't reward your dog for being excited by responding enthusiastically to them. Keep arrivals low-key to prevent increasing their anxiety about when you'll return. When you are at home, crate your dog for short periods so they don't link crating with being left alone.

Step 4, Part II: Crate your dog at night.

Use your regular command and a treat to encourage your dog to enter the crate. If you have a puppy, you might want to keep the crate in your bedroom or a neighboring corridor at first. Puppies regularly need to go out to relieve themselves late at night, and you'll want to be able to hear your dog alert you to let him out. To prevent associating the box with social isolation, older dogs should be kept out at first.

Once your dog is sleeping soundly in the crate near you at night, you can gradually move it to the desired location, though any time spent with your dog—even sleep time—is a chance to fortify your bond.

IS YOUR PUPPY WHINING IN HIS CRATE

While there is no perfect way to totally eliminate whining behavior in pups, there are strategies to reduce it. It's critical to perform good crate training and avoid instilling undesirable habits in your dog early on.

Below are a few things you can do to help your puppy stop whining in his crate.

Don't pay attention to the whining.

One of the most common mistakes novice pet parents make is paying attention to their puppies or taking them out of the crate once they start whining. The best choice is to ignore whining. Any attention will just serve to reinforce the behavior.

Pet parents should wait until a puppy is quiet before giving him attention or letting him out of the crate. The idea is to teach the puppy that calm, quiet behavior leads to a reward. After waking up from his nap or a few minutes of peaceful behavior, the puppy can be released.

Choose the appropriate crate size.

Puppies should have enough room in their crates to feel safe and secure. The dog must have the ability to stand up, turn around, and play with toys in the crate.

Consider dog crates with dividers so you can change the size of the crate as your puppy gets bigger.

Make your dog feel at ease in the crate.

One technique to lessen whimpering and anxiety in your puppy is to familiarize him with his crate.

The first rule is to introduce your dog to the crate gradually. Your puppy needs time to learn that the crate is a safe and happy place. If you start crating without giving him enough time to get to know you, he'll be more likely to object.

Never use the crate to punish your puppy. Treats, chew toys, and blankets in the crate will make the experience easier.

When your puppy is peaceful and quiet in his crate, praise him with dog treats. Most dogs will enter the crate on their own once they've become accustomed to it, so we recommend leaving the crate door open while it's not in use.

It becomes their secure refuge where they can relax, chew on toys, and watch their families.

Make sure there are lots of potty   breaks.

Puppies are unable to "hold it" for as long as adult dogs, thus it is the job of the pet parent to ensure that young puppies have plenty of opportunities to go outside—even in the middle of the night.

Kennel soiling is frequently induced by leaving the puppy alone for an extended period of time. To know the number of hours a puppy needs between potty breaks, add his age plus one.

A two-month-old puppy can normally hold it for three hours, while a three-month-old dog can usually hold it for four hours.

It's better to be safe than sorry, so estimate how long your puppy can go between potty breaks based on his age. When it comes to potty training, there is no such thing as too many trips outside.

Don't forget to think about the crate location.

The position of your puppy's crate may influence whether or not he whines. Crate placement has a significant impact on a dog's response to it. If the crate is positioned in a distant room, or even worse, the garage or basement, the puppy may feel isolated and cry.

The box should be kept where the family spends a lot of time. Some pet parents choose to utilize two crates, one in the family room or living room and the other in the puppy's bedroom.

Keeping the crate handy will allow you to hear when your puppy wants to go outside and make your puppy feel less nervous.

Because most young pups can't hold it for the entire night, pet parents must be able to hear when their puppies wake up and cry to go outside. Otherwise, the puppy may be compelled to soil the crate.

Allow your puppy to have plenty of opportunities to run about.

Don't underestimate the power of playtime to keep your puppy from whining in the crate.

In addition to the kennel, make sure your puppy is getting plenty of activity and attention. If this is the case, your dog will most likely be ready for a nap while crated.

To keep your puppy occupied and avoid boredom, add interactive or dog treat toys to his or her box. When you crate your dog, give him a safe, hard, rubber busy toy loaded with a little peanut butter or a few goodies. This tasty routine, if followed consistently, may help your puppy enjoy going into the crate.

Pet parents can try a KONG puppy dog toy, but we recommend testing toys first to ensure your dog won't rip them up.

WHEN TO WORRY ABOUT A PUPPY CRYING IN HIS CRATE

While puppy whining is common, whether a dog is crated or not, pet parents should be aware of any excessive whining or unusual behavior.

If whining is new behavior for a dog who has previously handled being crated well, or if you detect any other concerning signs, contact your veterinarian.

We agree that pet caregivers should be vigilant and seek assistance if puppy crying persists. Some puppy whining in the kennel is normal. It's critical to contact a trainer or veterinary behaviorist if a puppy is reactive the entire time he's crated—no matter how long he's been there—or hurts himself in an attempt to escape.

CHAPTER FOUR

RULE 4: SOCIALIZE A PUPPY TO GET AN OBEDIENT, CALM, AND SAFE DOG IN FUTURE

The first 8-12 weeks of your puppy's life define his future. The goal of socialization is to teach your puppy that the world is a safe place with kind people and dogs and that new experiences don't have to be frightening. It all depends on the proper handling of pups throughout their exciting first three months of existence.

When a puppy is exposed to new sights and sounds in a positive manner, he will become smarter, healthier, and more confident as an adult. To put it another way, he'll take things like hearing a garbage truck or climbing high stairs in stride.

The key to having a confident, happy, and well-adjusted dog is to socialize your puppy. In this chapter, you will learn the best time to socialize your puppy, why it's necessary, and how to do it correctly.

WHEN SHOULD YOUR PUPPY BE SOCIALIZED?

Your puppy will undergo a socialization process during his first three months of life that will influence his future personality and how he reacts to his environment as an adult dog. Exposing him to a diverse range of people, places, and experiences results in a profound, long-term improvement in his attitude.

Socialization should begin before bringing your puppy home from a trustworthy breeder. In your puppy's first few weeks, gentle handling by the breeder is beneficial to the development of a pleasant, confident dog. Puppies may approach a person who is passively observing them as early as three weeks of age, so having a knowledgeable breeder who supports pleasant experiences with adults and children will help mold the puppy's adult behavior. Good breeders expose their puppies to safe indoor and outdoor environments, car rides, crates, sounds, scents, and gentle handling as they grow up.

WHY SHOULD YOU SOCIALIZE YOUR PUPPY?

The purpose of socialization is to help your puppy become acquainted to a wide range of sights, sounds, and smells in a positive way. By preventing a dog from getting fearful of things like children or riding in a car, proper socialization can contribute to the development of a well-mannered, happy companion.

Being well-adjusted and confident could potentially save your dog's life one day. Improper socialization, according to the American Veterinary Society of Animal Behavior, can lead to behavioral problems later in life. According to the organization's position statement on socialization, "behavioral problems, not infectious illnesses, are the leading cause of death in dogs under the age of three." Start going out with your dog after your vet says it's safe, and he'll learn to behave in a variety of situations and love meeting new people.

WAYS TO SOCIALIZE YOUR DOG WITH OTHER DOGS AND HUMAN BEINGS

We're just living in your golden retriever's world, but that doesn't mean your pal gets a pass on being prim and proper. Follow these measures to ensure that your dog is a good canine citizen.

1. Daily Walks Are Crucial

Taking your dog for a walk in a public area will help him become more at ease with the world and the people around him. The world becomes a little less scary once you've been around the block a few times, from the mailman to cars driving down the street.

Keep your canine companion on a short leash and get some exercise— there's a lot to see and smell. Take varied routes to give your companion the opportunity to meet new people and see a range of places.

2. Mix It Up

Allow your dog to interact with a wide range of people, from men and women to youngsters, to help him become accustomed to the idea of people (who are much bigger). If your dog only spends time with one person, he may become suspicious of everyone else; therefore it's critical to diversify your dog's social calendar and schedule meet-and-greets.

- If your dog appears to be terrified, be calm and confident. Don't push, but also don't make a big issue out of nervous behavior.

- Make sure people pet your dog in places where their hands can be seen, such as on his chest or chin.

- Give your dog pleasant associations with new people and experiences by using rewards.

- Return to the basics. A well-rounded pooch is one that is confident in their training and routine.

- Hire a dog walker or a drop-in pet sitter to expose your dog to a variety of caregivers throughout the day.

3. Be Timely

The best time to socialize a puppy is between the ages of 3 and 12. During this critical period, your puppy should be exposed to a variety of events.

New puppies should often be exposed to:

- Unfamiliar faces

- Unfamiliar clothing (hoods, jackets, hats, and sunglasses)

- Body handling (paws, ears, tail, and so on)

- Vehicles

- Different types of flooring and ground surfaces

- Common neighborhood objects such as street signs, bicycles, strollers, skateboards, and benches

- Urban surroundings

- Parks, bodies of water, woodlands, and beaches

- Other dogs

- Cats

It becomes much more difficult to socialize a dog after 18 weeks (about four months)—but not impossible! Don't be discouraged if you have an older dog; you can teach an elderly dog new tricks.

4. Classes for Dogs

A little boot camp—or puppy kindergarten, for that matter—never harmed anyone. Ask your veterinarian about dog socialization options in your area that might be a suitable fit for you and your pet.

Dog training sessions are also a terrific way to meet new people and dogs in a safe and regulated setting.

HOW DO YOU INTRODUCE YOUR DOG TO OTHER DOGS?

Stock up on Treats

Because most dogs would do anything for a reward, having a supply at hand will help keep your dog on his best behavior. What do you do when your puppy has a successful interaction with another dog? Give him a treat, of course! This promotes good social conduct.

Delicious, high-value snacks will last longer—my dog loves freeze-dried raw treats, but only you know your dog's tastes.

String cheese, cooked chicken bits, or small pieces of a hard-boiled egg are all common dog treats. Simply modify your dog's calorie intake at dinner to offset the extra calories consumed at snack time.

Visit a Dog Park—or a Pet Store

Allow your bushy-tailed pal to do a lap around the park and make the rounds. If you're confident in your recall, go to an off-leash park or arrange a playdate with a friend's dog.

If you're out of compostable poop bags or that wonderful-smelling doggie shampoo, take your dog to the store to see what's new. He might make a new acquaintance! You're also likely to meet other dog owners in your area, which can lead to puppy playdates in the future.

Pay attention to your dog's signals.

Ensure interactions are long enough to get to know your companion but not so long that they tire him out.

It's the same with you and your best friend: spend too much time together, and you'll start to notice things you didn't see before...for better or worse.

Caution is advised.

Introducing a three-pound Chihuahua to a Great Dane may seem cute, but always be cautious when mixing dogs.

Before enabling a meet and sniff, make sure the other party is friendly. Recognize the indicators of your dog's distress (excessive panting, yawning, tail between the legs) and respond appropriately.

Remember that practice makes perfect, and the more effective interactions your dog has with his companions, the easier it will become.

THE TRUTH ABOUT PUPPY SOCIALIZATION AND HOW TO DO IT RIGHT

Puppies go through a "critical socializing period" between three and sixteen weeks. Puppies are sponges for the first three months of their existence, absorbing knowledge about the world as fast as it is offered to them.

When you're a puppy parent, socialization is your most crucial responsibility, and you should start socializing your puppy right away. Remember, your sponge window has been reduced to less than two months by the time they arrive with you!

Things, people, and places

Most people think of socialization as training a dog to get along with other dogs and people. While these factors are important in raising a well-adjusted dog, socialization entails exposing your puppy to all of the sights and sounds in their environment in a safe and beneficial manner.

- This may involve getting used to busy streets and automobile noise, loud buses, and skateboarders for city dwellers (or anybody planning regular visits to a city during their dog's life of 12+ years).

- Car rides (and a crate), bodies of water, and escalators are crucial to travelers.

- Farm animals and loud machinery may be acceptable to families that live in more rural areas.

Men, particularly those wearing hats, hoods, or sunglasses, should be considered, as well as children of all ages, canes or wheelchairs can create menacing images.

Small steps

The goal is to avoid overwhelming your puppy right away.

It's normal for a puppy to be scared the first time they encounter something unfamiliar. They may exhibit their fear by trembling, whining, tucking their tails, yawning, lip licking, or hiding or fleeing.

Keep the experience as enjoyable as possible for your dog by talking them through it and rewarding them with small bites of excellent food.

If your dog becomes distressed, move away from the socializing object or to a less intense version of it. If a busy street is too noisy for your puppy during his first socialization phase, consider a side street.

Vaccination schedules

You can still take your puppy out if it isn't fully immunized. Your puppy can still be socialized without having to put his feet on the ground. Most pups are small enough to be carried in a bag or your arms.

Your puppy can join you in public areas as long as you place a blanket or towel on the ground first. Ensure your puppy is kept on a leash, so they don't get too far away from the blanket.

The puppy social

The "puppy social" is another important aspect of puppy socialization. Puppy socials provide a safe setting for puppies to interact with other canines.

Most puppy socials allow puppies to play shortly after their second round of shots, because all puppies receive the same vaccinations (typically around 10 to 12 weeks of age).

Your dog will develop social skills at a social! If you are choosing between many puppy social options, choose one that is managed by a professional dog trainer who can help your puppy develop healthy play skills, shield them from unpleasant experiences, and educate you on how to do the same.

Supervision is required.

Two small creatures got into a serious struggle at one puppy social I helped supervise, and when we eventually managed to separate them, one pup was covered in blood. We dog trainers rushed into action, one comforting the injured dog and attempting to shift the situation from negative to positive while assessing the wounds; the other told the remaining dog guardians to gather their puppies and redirect their panic into good training behaviors.

Meanwhile, we awaited the veterinarian's approval and the aggressor's evacuation. This is an unusual occurrence with puppies, but it does happen. I fear to imagine how the attack might have affected the pup if there had been no qualified dog trainers present.

Your puppy can play with adult dogs belonging to friends and family members as long as they are completely vaccinated.

Always supervise interactions with dogs of any kind, and take a break if the adult grows irritated or overpowers the puppy.

CHAPTER FIVE

RULE 5: UNDERSTAND THE REASON TO SOLVE AND PREVENT A PUPPY'S PROBLEMATIC BEHAVIOR

Dog owners commonly mishandle or misunderstand behavioral issues in dogs. Maybe you're new to dog ownership, thinking about getting a puppy, or simply want to assist your dog with a problem. Understanding and preventing the most prevalent canine behavioral issues begins with understanding them thoroughly. Many of these issues can be controlled or avoided with a firm foundation of obedience training.

TEN REASONS WHY YOUR DOG MAY EXPERIENCE BEHAVIOR ISSUES

Whether you're training a new puppy or an older dog, a good foundation in positive training can get you off to a fantastic start. However, if there are any undesired canine behaviors present, training must be more than just a foundation. When it comes to behavioral issues, look at the big picture and study the most prevalent reasons why a dog "behaves badly." The first step in solving and preventing behavioral problems is understanding the most pervasive explanations.

1. Insufficient Exercise

Dogs require physical activity to be happy, and on-leash walks around the block are rarely enough. Off-leash runs, running behind you on a Walky Dog Bicycle or Springer bike leash, fetch games, a pole toy like a Chase-It, or dog-dog play/daycare for social dogs are good options.

2. Insufficient Mental Stimulation

Mental stimulation is important for a well-balanced dog, yet it is often overlooked. Mental exercise can be equally as exhausting as physical activity; a gardener might be just as fatigued at the end of the day as someone who works at a desk job. Using your dog's daily rations for enrichment activities or a small training session can help to mentally exhaust your dog. Enrichment activities can be as basic as hiding your dog's food or spreading it throughout the yard. Dogs enjoy foraging or working for their food.

3. Health Issues

Health difficulties generate behavioral problems more frequently than individuals realize; health concerns are frequently overlooked. Consider this: if you're not feeling well, you're likely to be irritable or unresponsive. Your dog is the same way, but a dog cannot communicate with you through words. Arthritis, hip dysplasia, luxating patellas, painful teeth, thyroid problems, epilepsy/seizures, ear infections, digestive disorders, skin or environmental allergies, yeast infections, hearing loss, loss of eyesight, and cancer are health conditions that might affect your dog's behavior. Contact your veterinarian if you see sudden hostility or any other behavioral issue. Any of the above health issues, or associated symptoms, could be the source of your dog's irritability.

4. Genetic Problems

Genetic factors can play a role in behavioral disorders. Aggression and hyperactivity are examples of behaviors that your dog may have inherited from his parents. When purchasing a puppy, it is critical to determine whether the parents have a positive temperament. If they don't, your puppy's chances of having a bad disposition are very high. You can sometimes overcome poor genetics with excellent socialization, but even the best socialization program will not solve behavior problems if your dog has lost the gene pool lottery. Genetic disorders usually manifest themselves at an early age and are difficult to treat.

5. Unpredictable Environment

Is it fair to let your dog jump on you when you're dressed casually, but discipline him for jumping other times? Dogs have no concept of clothing styles! This pattern, or lack thereof, is perplexing to him and might lead to anxiety. It reinforces jumping or any other activities that are consistently rewarded. If you want your dog to stop doing something, communicate with him in a consistent manner. For example, if your dog leaps, practice sitting with positive reinforcement (giving something your dog enjoys, such as treats or play, immediately after the activity) and entirely ignore your dog if he jumps. Ignoring your dog entails no talking, stroking, or eye contact, as these activities all need attention and might reinforce undesirable behavior. Turn your back on your dog and cross your arms until all four paws are on the ground.

Look in the mirror if your dog has a behavioral issue. How do you react? There's a good chance you've been rewarding the behavior with attention, and you may have even trained your dog to perform it! Barking is another example of reinforced undesirable behavior. Dog barks, you yell, and the dog believes you're barking too—look at how much attention I got! The dog barks more, you reprimand more, the dog barks more, and so on.

Your dog will understand that the environment is predictable if you have a regular set of boundaries and rules in your home. It also demonstrates to your dog that you provide leadership, guidance, and access to wonderful things. Allow your dog to learn the rules with patience and positive reinforcement. It requires time, consistency, and knowledge of what to ignore and reward to teach your dog not to leap up and to eliminate unwanted behavior.

6. Misconceptions about "Normal" Dog Behavior

Barking, pulling on the leash, eating excrement, rolling in dead things, jumping up to welcome, and guarding food and bones (to some extent) are all normal dog behaviors. Dogs growl when they feel threatened, chew whatever they can get their mouths on, pee and poop wherever, nip, protect the property or their family, herd, chase, and occasionally kill small animals. All of these "annoying" habits are entirely normal components of a dog's repertoire, and they differ by breed. Choose a dog breed that will fit your lifestyle. Getting a mastiff and being surprised when he growls at strangers approaching your home is simply unfair. These canines have been bred as guard dogs for thousands of years. Off-leash, Siberian huskies and northern breeds may be untrustworthy and kill small animals. Border Collies might herd your children. Dachshunds are known for their excessive barking. These characteristics are the result of job-specific breeding or natural canine behavior. You can occasionally train an alternative behavior, and other times you can't. It depends on how hardwired the behavior is genetically.

7. Routine Changes

Changing your dog's routine can be unpleasant and lead to behavioral problems. Dogs, like humans, want a sense of safety. Changes in their environment or habits might throw them off, generating worry that manifests in troublesome behavior. Moving to a new home frequently results in a gap in house training, among other problems. A new pet joining the family might be stressful for your dog, as can a change in work schedule. Be patient with your dog and treat him with kindness as he adjusts to change.

8. Dietary Changes

Changing your dog's diet to a lower-quality or less-suitable one can also make him act out. Diet significantly impacts behavior (going back to health influencing behavior). Changing your dog's diet to something low-quality or unsuitable for him may impact how he behaves. Always offer a high-quality diet to your dog, and switch foods gradually over the week or so.

9. Negative Socialization or Poor Socialization

As stated in the previous chapter, socialization means exposing your puppy to other canines, people of all types, sounds, surfaces, and new experiences in a positive and regulated manner. Dogs must be socialized with humans from when they are puppies and throughout their lives. The age from 3 to 16 weeks is essential for socialization. This period builds the groundwork for a balanced dog. If a puppy does not receive adequate socialization during this crucial period, he may grow up to be shy, fearful, or violent as an adult. A well-run puppy session can be a fun way to get your dog's socialization skills off on the right foot.

Even a well-socialized dog might acquire behavioral issues as a result of bad experiences. When your dog is assaulted by other dogs or mocked by youngsters while out in the yard, it can have a detrimental impact on his behavior. A bad visit to the veterinarian, training class, or groomer might have the same effect. Choose carefully where you take your dog to socialize and which professionals you entrust with his or her care. I would also advise you not to leave your dog alone in the yard when you are not at home, because you never know what may happen.

10. Adolescence or Fear Periods

Don't be alarmed if your ordinarily brave puppy becomes timid one day. As their brains mature, pups will go through numerous phases of dread. The first occurs between the ages of 8 and 12 weeks, and the second between the 5 and 6 months. Depending on your dog's breed and pedigree, he or she may have more or fewer fear periods. Do not be alarmed; simply allow your puppy to go through this stage. For a week, avoid going to the vet, training class, groomer, or any new places until your dog has returned to his normal behavior. Something that frightens your dog during a fear stage imprint very deeply. Rather than attempting to overcome a fear, it may be wiser to simply let it pass.

Adolescence begins around the age of 6 months and lasts between 12 and 18 months. Most dogs are surrendered to shelters throughout their adolescence. This is the time when puppies begin to explore their surroundings and test their limits. A formerly "good" dog may turn into a nightmare. During this time, continued obedience training, maintaining structure and boundaries, patience, and expert management are all necessary activities. When you can't oversee the dog personally, management implies setting up the environment so the dog doesn't get a chance to engage in "bad" activities. It also includes strategies like crating the dog.

Target to change

Understanding the most prevalent reasons for problematic behavior in dogs will help you figure out what's going on with your own difficult canine. Eliminate all probable sources of change. If feasible, reduce them down to a single trigger for your pet's unwanted behavior. You'll have a higher chance of swiftly eradicating the annoying behavior if you have more precise details. Of course, if your dog's behavioral issues are severe, you should seek the assistance of a competent trainer.

10 COMMON DOG BEHAVIOR PROBLEMS AND SOLUTIONS

As dog owners, there is something we must comprehend. Most, if not all, of the listed behavioral issues, are common in dogs to some extent. However, there are several options for reducing or stopping this tendency.

Why are simple behaviors like chewing or play biting such a big deal? They can become excessive if left unaddressed. In the examples below, you'll see what I mean.

Let's talk about some of the most frequent dog behavior issues, starting with the one that everyone hates: barking.

1. Barking

The majority of dogs communicate in some form. They may bark, howl, or whine, among other things. Excessive barking is considered a behavioral issue.

Determine why your dog is vocalizing in the first place before you can correct barking. The following are the most typical barking behaviors:

- Playfulness and excitement
- Warning or alert
- Attention-seeking
- Boredom
- Anxiety
- Responding to other dogs

Control their excessive barking. Consider teaching them commands like bark/quiet. Maintain consistency and patience. Any underlying reasons for barking should be addressed. Barking dogs can be controlled with dedication and attention to detail.

2. Chewing

Chewing comes naturally to all dogs. In reality, it is an important habit for most dogs; it's just how they're wired. Excessive chewing, however, can rapidly turn into a behavioral issue if your dog destroys things. Below are the most common reasons dogs chew:

- Boredom or excess energy

- Puppy teething

- Anxiety

- Curiosity

To convince your dog to chew on appropriate things, provide plenty of suitable chew toys. Keep your items out of your dog's reach. When you're not at home, keep your dog confined or crated to an area where less destruction can occur.

If you see your dog gnawing on anything inappropriate, distract him with a loud noise. After that, a chew toy should be substituted for the inappropriate item. One of the most significant things to do for your dog is to make sure he receives lots of exercise to burn off energy and be stimulated instead of chewing.

3. Digging

When given the opportunity, most dogs will dig to some extent; it's instinctive. Because of their origins as hunters, some dog breeds, such as terriers, are more prone to digging. Most dogs dig for the following reasons:

- Anxiety or fear

- Boredom or excess energy

- Hunting instinct

- Desire to hide possessions (like toys or bones)

- Comfort-seeking (such as cooling off or nesting)

- To gain access or escape from an area

It can be very frustrating f your dog digs up your yard. Determine what is causing the digging and then seek to eradicate the source. More exercise, quality time with your dog, and extra training are all things you should do. If digging seems unavoidable, set aside an area where your dog can dig freely, such as a sandbox. Teach your dog that digging is only allowed in this specific region.

4. Anxiety about Separation

One of the most common behavioral issues in puppies is separation anxiety. When a dog is removed from his owner, he may exhibit vocalization, chewing, incontinence (urinating and defecating), and other destructive behaviors. All of these behaviors aren't caused by separation anxiety.

Signs of actual separation anxiety include:

- The dog becomes apprehensive as the owner prepares to leave

- Misconduct occurs within 15 to 45 minutes of the owner's departure

- The dog constantly follows the owner around

- The dog attempts to touch the person whenever possible

True separation anxiety necessitates extensive instruction, behavioral change, and desensitization exercises. In extreme circumstances, medication may be prescribed.

5. Inappropriate Urination and Defecation

The most irritating dog behavior is incontinence. It can damage your property and make your dog unpleasant in public places or at other people's houses. It's crucial to speak to your vet about this habit to rule out any health issues. If no medical cause can be established, try to figure out what's causing the behavior, which could be one of the following:

- Territorial marking

- Anxiety

- Lack of adequate housebreaking

- Submissive/excitement urinating

In pups, especially before the age of 12 weeks, inappropriate urination and defecation are unavoidable. It's a different story with older pets. Many dogs need extensive behavior training to break the habit once it has developed.

6. Begging

Although begging is a terrible habit, many dog owners encourage it. This might result in digestive issues as well as obesity. Dogs crave food because they enjoy it. Table scraps, on the other hand, are not treats, and food is not affection. Yes, it's difficult to resist that wistful gaze, but giving in "just once" causes a long-term problem. You're sending the wrong message to your dog by teaching him that begging is OK.

Before sitting down to eat, tell your dog to go to his spot, preferably somewhere he won't be able to see you. If necessary, separate your dog from the rest of the house. If he behaves, reward him with a special treat once you and your family are done eating.

7. Chasing

The urge of a dog to chase moving objects is merely a manifestation of predatory instinct. Many dogs chase other dogs, people, and automobiles. All of these features are likely to be disastrous. While you may find it hard to stop your dog from chasing, there are steps you can take to avert disaster.

- Always keep your dog contained or on a leash (unless directly supervised indoors).

- Teach your dog to respond to commands.

- Keep an eye out for possible triggers, such as joggers.

- Keep a dog whistle or noisemaker handy to attract your dog's attention.

Your best chance of succeeding is to keep the chase under control. Devoted training over the course of your dog's life will teach him to initially focus on you before running away.

8. Jumping Up

In dogs, jumping up is a typical and natural activity. Puppies leap to their feet to welcome their mothers. They may likewise jump up when greeting others. Dogs may jump up when they are enthusiastic or looking for something in a person's hands. A jumping dog can be irritating and dangerous.

There are several ways to deter a dog from jumping, but not all of them will work. Lifting a knee, grabbing the dog's paws, or pushing the dog away may be helpful, but it sends the wrong message to most dogs. Because jumping up is a common attention-seeking behavior, acknowledging your dog's activities is an instant reward for jumping.

Simply turning aside and ignoring your dog is the most effective strategy. If necessary, take a step back. Don't look at, talk to, or pet your dog. Continue with what you are doing. When he relaxes and remains immobile, reward him quietly. It won't be long before your dog comprehends what you're saying.

9. Biting

Dogs nip and bite for various reasons, most of which are instinctive. Puppies pinch and bite to investigate their surroundings. Mother dogs educate their puppies to bite gently and reprimand them when necessary. This aids the development of biting inhibition in puppies. By continuing to teach bite inhibition, owners can show their puppies that mouthing and biting are not acceptable.

Dogs bite for a variety of causes, including puppy behavior. Biting or snapping is not always motivated by aggression. A dog may snap, nip, or bite for various reasons.

- Defensiveness
- Fear
- Protection of property
- Predatory instinct
- Pain or sickness

Any dog may bite if the conditions in the dog's head justify it. Through correct training, socialization, and breeding procedures, owners and breeders can help reduce the likelihood of biting.

10. Adversity

Growling, flashing teeth, snarling, lunging, and biting are all signs of dog aggression. It's important to understand that any dog, regardless of history or breed, has the potential to be aggressive. Dogs with violent or abusive histories, as well as those bred from aggressive dogs, are significantly more prone to display aggressive behavior toward people or other dogs.

Unfortunately, some breeds are classified as "dangerous" and prohibited in some locations. It's usually not so much about the breed as it is about history. The environment has a significant impact on a dog's behavior. A dog may also inherit aggressive tendencies regardless of breed. Thankfully, the majority of experts believe that breed-specific laws are not the solution.

The reasons for aggression are similar to the reasons a dog bites or snaps; however, canine aggression is a far more serious issue. If your dog is acting aggressively, see your veterinarian right away because it could be a sign of a health condition. Then, enlist the assistance of a professional dog trainer or behaviorist. To keep others safe from aggressive dogs, serious precautions should be taken.

CHAPTER SIX

RULE 6: USE POSITIVE REINFORCEMENT

A dog may bring a lot of happiness into your life. However, obedience training is an important aspect of socializing dogs. f you do not provide proper training, your dog will find it difficult to integrate with your family and friends, as well as other canines.

This might be difficult or embarrassing in some instances. And it could have disastrous repercussions in extreme circumstances.

As a responsible dog owner, it is your responsibility to ensure that your dog is properly trained. You should enroll your puppy in obedience classes as soon as possible. Your dog will be much more open to instruction and have a better potential for learning throughout this period of his life.

Obedience lessons are also an excellent way for your dog to gain socialization with other dogs. Below, we've outlined all of the reasons why training your dog is critical.

It Instils Life Skills in Your Dog

You equip your dog with the abilities he needs to live peacefully among humans and other animals by teaching him properly. You might think that domestic dogs have it easier than their wild counterparts. However, living in a human family places pressure on your dog, which it must learn to manage.

If you don't train your dog properly, he may develop destructive habits. When you're not around, he can become agitated and chew up your furniture. They may also be aggressive toward people or other animals.

Stress Reduction

You're harming your dog in the long term if you fail to properly train him. Well-trained dogs are often calm and comfortable and can blend well with humans.

However, if your dog has not been properly trained, he may become aggressive and fearful. If your dog exhibits worrying tendencies, you can help by reassuring him.

If he's afraid of visitors, you might put up a baby gate to separate him from them. You might also simply relocate them to a different room.

On the other hand, if your dog is very excited and jumps up at visitors, you should teach him how to appropriately welcome visitors without being so boisterous. It's critical to address these issues as soon as possible, as they could endanger the dog or other people.

It Aids in Conflict Avoidance

It's critical that your dog has socialization experience with both humans and animals. If your dog is not relaxed around other animals, it may cause conflict and even injury to your dog or another pet.

It's simply not possible to keep your dog away from other animals all of the time. Your dog will inevitably encounter other dogs at some point. Your dog should socialize with other animals on a regular basis to avoid nervousness or hostility with other animals.

Taking your puppy to obedience training while they're still young is a terrific approach to accomplish this. This does not necessarily imply that your dog must enjoy playing with other animals. Some dogs prefer not to play with other dogs.

Your dog simply needs to be at ease in the presence of other animals, with no symptoms of hostility or worry. If your dog does not get this kind of exposure, he or she may respond aggressively when coming into contact with other animals.

It might assist you in comprehending your dog.

Dog training entails much more than simply educating your pet. It can also assist you in getting to know your dog's needs better.

There are several half-truths out there when it comes to dog training. Many individuals unintentionally cause anxiety in their dogs without even realizing it.

You can be sure you're getting good guidance when you go to dog obedience training.

When you leave your dog alone, he will behave.

Leaving a dog alone might be one of the most challenging aspects of dog ownership. You'll have to leave your dog alone at home at some point. When that time arrives, you must have faith in their ability to behave responsibly.

Untrained dogs may growl and wail for hours or chew up anything they can get their paws on. This type of behavior might be pricey and can also lead to noise complaints being filed against you.

When a dog exhibits these actions, it indicates that he is in a bad mood. When you properly educate your dog from a young age, it reinforces good behavior patterns and lowers separation anxiety.

Most of the time, a dog that misbehaves when left alone may be taught to behave appropriately with proper obedience training.

It'll Make Your Dog More Secure

A dog that refuses to obey commands is in danger. There are many dangers in the world that dogs may not be aware of.

A dog, for example, does not comprehend the concept of a road. If your dog ignores commands, he or she may rush into the road and get hit by a car.

A well-trained dog is safe from most dangers because he can be directed to avoid them. Teaching your dog to sit and wait before crossing the road is a smart idea. When your dog has learned this behavior, they will repeat it even if they are separated from you.

WHAT IS POSITIVE REINFORCEMENT?

Training dogs (and other animals) using positive reinforcement is very effective. Positive reinforcement refers to doing something immediately after a behavior occurs to increase the frequency of that behavior.

The phrase is technically broken down into two pieces. Reinforcement occurs when a behavior is repeated or increased in frequency (it is not reinforcement if the behavior decreases).

Positive implies that something has been added.

For instance, you instruct the dog to sit, he sits, and you reward him with a treat (something is added). When you ask the dog to sit again, he is more likely to do so (the behavior was reinforced).

IN POSITIVE REINFORCEMENT, WHAT KIND OF REWARD IS USED?

Food is the best incentive for most dog training. It is efficient and effective because all dogs appreciate food, and it can be provided quickly.

In dog training, play is sometimes utilized as a reward. A round of tug-of-war or fetch, for example. You may have even seen working or agility dogs being rewarded with a round of tug-of-war.

Food is the most effective method for most dog training scenarios. You can deliver it faster (think about how long it takes to play a round of tug-of-war versus how long it takes your dog to eat a treat). That implies you can immediately perform another repetition. Furthermore, the play might sometimes get in the way of what you're trying to teach.

Petting and praise have been offered as rewards in the past. However, it helps to consider it from the dog's perspective - and indeed, scientists have considered it as well. According to one study, dogs seem uninterested in praise. It needs to be conditioned to be meaningful. If "good boy" is always accompanied by a reward, for example, they will learn it means "treat," but otherwise, it means nothing.

Although most dogs enjoy being petted, the same researchers discovered that dogs prefer food to stroke as a reward in dog training. Other studies have compared food to petting as a reward in a dog training context, if you're curious. They also discovered that eating leads to improved results.

The issue of efficiency is also relevant: food is prepared faster. As a result, food is the best positive reinforcement reward.

HOW TO TRAIN YOUR DOG THE 5 BASIC COMMANDS WITH POSITIVE REINFORCEMENT

To get off on the right foot (and paw!) with your dog, make sure he understands what you expect of him. This will give him confidence in his capacity to achieve the objectives set for him.

Positive reinforcement should be the cornerstone of training. Positive reinforcement refers to rewarding a dog (or person!) for doing the desired behavior, such as getting paid for coming to work. The goal is to train the behavior through something your dog values, rather than bribery. Avoid yelling or leash corrections as forms of punishment. When a dog is punished, he may become confused and unclear about what is expected of him. We must remember that we cannot expect dogs to know what they do not know, just as we would not expect a 2-year-old child to know how to tie his shoes. Patience and tolerance will help toward teaching your new puppy proper behavior.

Anything your dog likes can be used as reinforcement. Most people use small portions of a "high value" meal, such as freeze-dried liver or even kibble, as training treats – something special. Lavish praise or the opportunity to play with a favorite toy can be used as a reward. Praise must be taught to dogs. Giving the dog a treat while saying "Good dog!" in a positive tone of voice will teach him that praise is good and can be used as a reward. Some dogs prefer being petted. Often, the most appropriate way to reinforce behavior is through food.

Puppies can begin basic training as soon as they arrive home, usually around the age of eight weeks. Always keep training sessions short (5 to 10 minutes) and end on a positive note. If your puppy is having problems learning a new behavior, end the session by going over something he already knows and reward him with plenty of praise and a huge treat. It will be harmful to learning if your puppy becomes bored or frustrated.

1. Teaching Your Dog to Come When Called

Start training a recall (come to you when called) in a quiet, indoor environment.

- Sit next to your dog and say "come" or his name.

- Give your puppy a treat every time you say "come/ name." He is not required to do anything at this time! Simply say the word again and offer a treat. Easy!

- Then, drop a treat on the floor close to you. Say your puppy's name once more when he eats the goodie on the ground. Give him another treat when he looks up.

- Do this several times until you can toss the treat a bit farther away and he turns around to face you when you call his name. Note: If you speak your puppy's name too often and he doesn't answer, it will become easier for him to ignore you. Instead, get closer to your puppy and return to a stage where he can reply to his name correctly the first time. Begin adding movement and making the game more fun once your dog can turn around to face you. Toss a treat on the ground and quickly back up while calling your puppy's name. They should chase you down because it's enjoyable to chase!

- Give your puppy lots of praise, food, or a tug toy when he catches you. Coming to you should be fun! Continue to improve these games by extending them across long distances and in different locales. When teaching your puppy outside (always in a safe, enclosed location), keep him on a long leash at first.

Don't reach out and grasp your dog when he comes to you. For some dogs, this can be perplexing or terrifying. If your dog is fearful, kneel down and face them sideways while reaching for the collar. Never call your dog to punish! This will simply educate him that you are unpredictable and that avoiding you is a good option. Even if your dog has been mischievous, always lavish praise on him or her for responding to his or her name.

2. How to Teach a Dog to Loose-Leash Walk

"Heel" refers to the dog walking on your left side with his head level with your knee as you hold the leash lightly in competition obedience training. Puppy training can be more laid-back, with the goal of walking respectfully on a slack leash without pulling. When teaching this simple manner of walking together, some trainers prefer to say "let's go" or "forward" rather than "heel."

Whatever cue you use, be consistent and use the same term every time. It is entirely up to you whether your puppy walks on your left or right side. However, be consistent with where you want them to go, so they don't become confused and start zigzagging in front of you.

- Make sure your dog feels at ease when on a leash. At first, this may seem unusual, and some puppies may bite the leash. As you put on the leash each time, give your puppy treats.

- Then, with the leash in a loose loop, stand next to your puppy and offer him many treats in a row for standing or sitting next to your leg.

- Take a step forward and reward him for catching up by giving him another treat.

- As you go ahead, continue to give treats to your puppy at your knee or hip level.

- When he rushes in front of you, turn around, call him to you, and reward him where he is. Then proceed. Gradually increase the distance between treats (from every step to every other step, every third step, and so on).

- Eventually, when your dog is on his leash, he will cheerfully stroll with you. Allow plenty of time for your dog to sniff and "smell the roses" throughout your walks. Give the cue "Let's Go!" in a joyful voice when he has had his sniffing time, and reward him for getting back into position and walking with you.

3. Teaching a Dog to Sit

There are two approaches to teaching your dog what "sit" means.

The first technique is known as capturing.

- Hold some of your puppy's dog food or treats in front of him.

- When he takes a seat, say "yes" and give him a treat.

- Then, to urge him to stand, take a step backward or sideways and wait for him to sit.

- As soon as he sits, give him another treat.

- You can start saying "sit" right as he sits after a few repetitions.

The next option is known as luring.

- Get down in front of your puppy and tempt him with a treat.

- Place the reward directly in front of the dog's nose, then slowly lift it above his head. He'll most likely sit, lifting his head to chew on the reward.

- When his bottom contacts the ground, let him eat the treat.

- Repeat with the food lure one or two times, then remove the food and use only your empty palm to treat the puppy after he sits.

- You can start saying "sit" right before you deliver the hand signal once he learns the signal.

Never force your puppy to sit; this might be confusing or distressing for some pups.

4. Teaching a Dog to Lie Down

"Down" is taught similarly to "sit."

- Wait for your dog to lie down (starting in a small, boring area like a restroom can assist)

- Reinforce the behavior by rewarding your dog with a treat when he lies down

- Wait for him to lie down again after giving him his release cue to stand up (and encouragement with a lure if necessary).

- You can start saying "down" right before he lies down after standing up.

You can also lure a down from a standing or sitting position.

- Slowly bring a treat to the dog's nose while holding it in your hand.

- To begin, give the treat when the dog's elbows touch the floor.

- After a few repetitions, bring your empty hand to the floor and give the treat AFTER he lies down.

- Begin saying "down" as you move your hand when he can reliably follow your hand signal.

Never force your dog into a down, just as you would with a sit.

5. Teaching a Dog to Stay

A puppy who understands the "stay" command will remain seated until you give him another command, the "release word." Staying still is a long-term behavior. The impression is to get your dog to sit until the release cue is delivered, then gradually increase the distance.

- First, teach the term "release." Choose an appropriate term, such as "OK" or "free."

- Stand with your dog while he is sitting or standing, toss a treat on the floor, and say your command as he approaches it.

- Practice this several times until you can speak the word first, then toss the reward AFTER he moves. This teaches the dog that the release cue indicates that he should move his feet.

- Have your dog sit. Turn and face him, and give him a treat after he understands the release cue and how to sit on command.

- Take a moment to reward him for staying seated, then let him go.

- Gradually lengthen the time between treats (singing the ABCs in your head and working your way up the alphabet can help).

- It's fine if your dog gets up before the release cue! It simply implies he isn't ready to sit for that long, and you can make things easy by reducing the time.

- Once your dog can sit for several seconds, you can start increasing the distance.

- Have him sit and say "stay," then take a step back, return, give him a treat, and say "release."

- Gradually increase the difficulty while keeping it simple enough for your dog to succeed. Practice facing him and walking away with your back turned (which is more realistic).

You can gradually increase the distance once your dog can stay. This also applies to the command "sit." The more thoroughly he understands it, the longer he can sit. The key is not to have unrealistic expectations. Because progress is made in small steps, you may need to slow down and focus on one thing at a time. Sessions should be brief and effective to ensure that the training "sticks."

CHAPTER SEVEN

RULE 7: GOOD CARE WILL HELP KEEP A PUPPY HEALTHY

Dogs are unable to communicate their feelings to us. Anyone who has ever had a furry buddy understands how expressive canine body language can be. In the early stages of an illness, dogs will naturally disguise how they are feeling. You may be able to detect small changes in your dog's behavior and actions because you are familiar with them.

Something is usually amiss when these slight changes occur. The key to assisting your dog in recovering rapidly is recognizing a problem as soon as possible. Here are 11 warning signals that will help you assess whether or not your dog is unwell and needs medical care.

11 COMMON INDICATORS THAT YOUR DOG IS ILL AND NEEDS TO SEE A VETERINARY

Breeders are busy cleaning, weighing, handling, and much more while a litter or two is on the ground. With so much on their plate, it might be difficult to notice the first signs of a sick dog. Despite thorough research, new owners may be unaware of the symptoms of some illnesses or how a sick puppy may appear or behave. We've put together a simple checklist to assist breeders and new puppy owners in spotting early signs of disease.

1. Diarrhea or Vomiting

The most common causes for seeking the assistance of a veterinarian are vomiting and/or diarrhea, which are often the first signs of a dog's illness. The issue can be minor and transitory or serious and life-threatening. A change in diet, getting into the trash, viral or bacterial diseases, motion sickness, parvovirus in pups, or ingestion of a foreign object can cause these symptoms.

If your puppy has had an episode of diarrhea or vomiting due to an upset stomach and is acting normally, keep an eye on him for any worsening symptoms. For a day or two, a bland wet diet, such as boiled chicken or hamburger with rice, can be served in small amounts until symptoms subside.

After you've determined that your dog is no longer vomiting or experiencing loose stool, add dry food to the mix. Please contact your veterinarian if symptoms occur frequently across 24 hours and are accompanied by weakness, lethargy, a loss of appetite, or unproductive vomiting (dry heaves).

2. Increased or Decreased Urination

Housetrained dogs do not suddenly start urinating in the house. Keep the following signals in mind:

- Changes in urine volume (a decrease or increase)

- Straining to urinate

- Blood in the urine

These symptoms are particularly relevant in senior dogs. Urination that is very frequent could suggest a renal problem or diabetes. A urinary tract infection, bladder stones, a blood clot, or cancer can all cause bloody urine.

If you notice blood, or your dog is straining to urinate, or urinates frequently, schedule an appointment with your veterinarian. Take a urine sample with you if feasible.

3. Appetite Suppression

Most dogs have their own feeding routines, and they eat more on some days than others. Loss of appetite can be a sign of a variety of issues. Some are minor, while others are serious. Anorexia can suggest dental illness when it is accompanied by foul breath.

You can give your puppy their favorite treats or a small portion of cooked chicken or hamburger meat. If the condition persists for more than a day or is accompanied by additional symptoms such as lethargy, vomiting, or weakness, you should consult your veterinarian.

4. Habitual Changes in Drinking

Drinking more or less water than usual could indicate that your dog is sick. Drinking too little water can suggest that your pet isn't feeling well while drinking too much water can indicate a fever, hormone problems, diabetes, or kidney disease.

Keep track of your pet's water consumption. If they're not drinking as much as they should, consider placing more water bowls around the house or flavoring the water with chicken broth. Check to determine whether they are also urinating more. If the problem persists, consult your veterinarian and, if feasible, obtain a urine sample.

5. Unexpected Weight Gain or Loss

Sudden weight loss or gain could indicate a health problem. It may take a few weeks to see this symptom.

Unexplained weight gain or loss can be caused by a variety of factors and is always a cause for concern. The best thing to do is to have your dog assessed to determine the root of the problem.

6. Personality Changes

When dogs are uncomfortable or feeling unwell, they show behavioral changes including decreased activity or lethargy. Some sick dogs that are usually social may start to withdraw. A friendly and active pet may develop snippiness or hostility.

Observe whether your dog growls when you approach a part of the body that may be causing discomfort. Not all dogs will act aggressively when they are sick. Clinginess or symptoms of increasing neediness may develop in some dogs. Some just show changes in their routine, which is common in dogs suffering from canine cognitive impairment.

Additional signs to watch for include loss of appetite, abdominal pain, vomiting, diarrhea, lameness, and straining while urinating. Contact a licensed veterinarian if you detect severe changes in your dog's behavior or additional symptoms.

7. Coughing, wheezing, or breathing difficulties

Symptoms of a respiratory condition include coughing, wheezing, difficulty breathing, and nasal discharge. Symptoms might range from a simple cold to canine influenza, kennel cough, or heart failure. A honking noise could indicate tracheal collapse, which is prevalent in small dog breeds.

Consider it a medical emergency if your dog has trouble breathing or has a blue tint to his mouth and gums. An infrequent cough should be appropriately examined and investigated if it does not resolve or is accompanied by other symptoms. Any unexpected change in your dog's health could be life-threatening!

8. Itchy Skin/Hair Loss

Skin infections, fleas, or allergies can cause hair loss (alopecia) or persistent itching. This can be very uncomfortable.

Look for fleas, evidence of flea filth (which looks like fresh ground pepper), redness, discharge, swelling, soreness, or an unusual odor on your dog's skin. A bath can help with mild symptoms, but a veterinarian should check in case of more serious symptoms.

9. Difficulty/Stiffness/Lameness Rising

Arthritis, hip dysplasia, joint difficulties, infections like Lyme disease, or a broken bone can cause difficulty walking or limping.

If your pet is lame or stiff, limit their activities. If the symptom is minor and their behavior is otherwise normal, you may be able to give your dog a day off. Consult your vet if you are concerned or if the problem persists.

10. Changes in the Eyes

Red eyes, runny eyes, squinting, or closing the eye might indicate various issues, from a minor infection to an ulcer or glaucoma.

If your dog is pawing or touching his eyes, attempt to stop him and contact your veterinarian. Rubbing the eyes can be very harmful. In addition to medicine application as suggested by your veterinarian, you may require an e-collar.

11. Pale Gums

Lifting the lip and inspecting the gum tissue is the best approach to determine your dog's gum color. Gums in normal dogs are pink and wet. Dogs with pale gums could be anemic or be in shock. All potential causes could be dangerous.

It's a medical emergency if your dog's gums are pale, he's lethargic, weak, or has difficulties breathing. For immediate medical assistance, contact your veterinarian or the nearest veterinary emergency clinic.

HOW TO KEEP YOUR DOG IN SHAPE AND HEALTHY

Your puppy will count on you to keep him healthy. A healthy diet, frequent exercise, grooming, and visits to the veterinarian will keep your dog in peak condition. It's also crucial to know your dog's behaviors, such as sleeping, eating, drinking, etc. A change in those habits can indicate that he's not feeling well.

These recommendations will maintain your dog's or cat's peak health, from correct nutrition and preventative meds to grooming and mental stimulation.

1. Adequate nourishment.

Feeding your pet the proper type and amount of food keeps him at a healthy weight, which is one of the best methods to avoid obesity-related issues and extend his life. A balanced diet of high-quality food can usually meet your pet's nutritional needs but check with your veterinarian to determine if any supplements are required. According to most vets, you should make sure your puppy has plenty of fresh water and keep the number of treats you give him to no more than 10% of his daily caloric intake. Consult a veterinarian for assistance.

2. Work out.

Regular walks, playing fetch, hiking, and swimming help keep your pet fit and active. However, don't overlook mental stimulation! Playing with toys, hiding goodies, creating obstacle courses, and performing new tricks keep your dog happy and involved. You can also alter your walking routine to give your pet new sights and smells.

3. Regular checkups

Your veterinarian can perform several health tests during a yearly wellness visit, which can help to detect diseases and warning signs of serious illness early. Plaque and tartar buildup may require yearly dental treatments to be removed.

4. Medication for prevention.

Preventative measures and regular veterinarian checks go hand in hand. Preventive medications can help you avoid heartworm, flea-related illnesses, and tick-borne infections. Periodontal disease can lead to severe health problems and be prevented by brushing your pet's teeth and feeding him dental chews regularly.

5. Personal hygiene.

Brushing your pet once or twice a week, trimming his nails, and bathing him on a regular basis are all part of the routine. Grooming can also help you spot dandruff, bald spots, or dry skin on your pet's fur or skin. It's also a good time to check for any lumps or bumps that might be concerning. To find the optimum grooming approach for your pet, consult your veterinarian.

6. Affection.

A solid bond with your dog is beneficial to both of you. Cuddles, petting, belly rubs, and even stroking his coat are all wonderful ways to express your affection for your dog. This not only fortifies your emotional bond with your pet, but also encourages pleasant interactions with other animals and people.

7. Socialization

Early socialization [in dogs] and adequate exposure to varied individuals and situations at a young age minimizes the risks of antisocial or fearfully aggressive behaviors as an adult. Puppies' formative years, which run from a few weeks old to about 16-18 weeks, are crucial for socialization. So, make sure they get enough human and animal interaction not just in the early months, but throughout their life. Options include visiting family and friends, going to dog parks, taking a walk around the neighborhood, or allowing your pet to spend an afternoon at daycare after being cleared by your veterinarian.

8. Neuter/spay.

There are various advantages to having your pet fixed. It can help your pet live longer, prevent various cancers and disorders, and reduce aggressive behavior in males. It can stop females from going into heat and lessen undesired cycle behaviors like irritation, yowling, and urine spraying.

9. Understand what is "normal."

Has your pet's behavior recently changed? Is he scratching more than he normally does? Is he eating more or less than he usually does? Changes from the norm could be alarming and indicate an underlying issue. If your dog exhibits unusual behavior, contact your veterinarian to see if an examination is required.

10. Pet protection.

Collars with ID tags, microchips, a risk-free environment, and keeping hazardous substances out of reach are ways to keep your pet safe. If you follow the other tips above, you'll be able to keep your furry buddy happy, healthy, and with you for many years.

WHEN SHOULD I TAKE MY DOG TO THE VET?

If your dog is displaying any of these non-emergency symptoms and you're still unsure whether or not to take him to the vet, trust your gut. You are the expert on your dog. Because abrupt changes are unsettling, you should act as you see fit.

Unfortunately, your pet will not approach you and inform you that they are ill. As a result, dog owners must recognize the early signs as soon as possible. Schedule an appointment with your veterinarian if your dog exhibits any of these symptoms if you want to know how to identify whether your dog is sick quickly and without guessing. Your veterinarian will inquire about your dog's medical history and may conduct tests.

Share your dog's medical history.

- Your veterinarian may request the following:

- Medical history of the dog, including any previous medical treatments

- Medications in use

- Symptoms that your dog is exhibiting. This includes when they first appeared, how often they occur, and other details.

CONCLUSION

Bringing a puppy home is one of life's greatest joys. Those two gleaming eyes would warm anyone's heart. Even if they belong to the small puppy that just ruined the kitchen...

You can yet have your cake and eat it!

You now have all the tools and strategies you need to teach your puppy and convert him into a well-behaved dog, thanks to everything you've learned in **7 Rules for The Perfect Puppy.**

Here are a few things you have learned:

- Recognizing your dog's body language

- Teaching your dog the five most crucial commands: "Sit," "Stay," "Lie Down," "Recall," and "Heel."

- Housebreaking and crate training, and

- Correcting negative behavior such as biting, jumping, and excessive barking

We've emphasized throughout this book that a dog is a social being who is genetically programmed to respond to humans and other dogs in both submissive and dominant ways. We've stressed the need to see yourself as your dog's guide and alpha figure, and include him in as many of your activities as possible. You should be able to enjoy creating a healthy relationship with your pet after you understand the significance of these concepts.

However, if you open yourself up to the possibilities, you can get a lot more out of your relationship with your dog. Your dog may give you unrivaled access to the natural world, assisting you in expanding your capacity for aesthetic appreciation, warmth, and delight, thereby anchoring you in more profound realities. We have dangerously lost touch with nature in an increasingly artificial and plastic world, and the result has been a wasteland of spiritual aridity and alienation. Most individuals have no idea that their relationship with their dog can lead to a more complete understanding of the cosmos.

Training your dog can be intimidating, especially if you're new to pet ownership. Whether you're a first-time dog owner or an experienced one, obedience training takes the same essential components: patience, effort, and consistency.

It can be a beautiful experience to take your dog to obedience training. When professional classes aren't an option, the DIY method might be a fun (and successful) alternative. The following is a synopsis of what this book teaches pet owners:

Consult your veterinarian.

Consult a veterinarian who has treated your dog before beginning your obedience-training adventures. Your veterinarian may be able to offer breed-specific advice on how to persuade your dog to comply. If your dog came from a shelter, has a medical issue, or is anxious, you may need to take a different approach to obedience training. Before you move on to the next phase, be sure you have all of your facts from an expert.

Invest in the correct tools.

You do not necessarily need to spend a lot to train your dog. However, you must begin with the proper materials. Include the following items in your dog training toolkit:

A short leash: Walking your dog on a short leash (four feet or less) to teach him appropriate behavior will make both of your lives much easier. You can progress to more sophisticated training on a longer leash once you've mastered the basics.

Small, nutritious dog treats: These can range in size from a small cheese stick to cereal-sized snacks tailored for training. Remember, the idea is to use small, readily digestible rewards that won't fill your dog up or make them sluggish before your obedience training sessions are through.

One active/engagement reward is required: After a successful training session, you can reward your dog with a game of tug-of-war, a few rounds of fetch, or a peanut butter-filled chew toy.

Start with the fundamentals.

Save the fancy stuff until later, even if you're ready to show off how brilliant your closest friend is. Four of the most funda-mental orders for teaching your dog to obey are "Come," "Sit," "Heel," and "Stay." These terms can create a common language that you and your dog can understand.

For two reasons, the "Come" command is an excellent place to start. Playing outside and spending time off-leash becomes safer for your dog once he or she understands how to come to you on command. Second, your dog is likely to come up to greet you many times throughout the day, so he or she may not require much coaxing.

Act as if it was your idea the next time your dog comes leaping up to you. Say their name, pause for a beat, and say, "Come!" Give your dog a treat for "responding," then back up and re-peat the instruction to see if they will do it again. It won't be long before your dog understands that obedience means reward. To avoid confusion, concentrate on memorizing one command at a time.

Teaching other commands will be much easier once your dog learns the notion of obedience. Say the order before physically moving your dog into a sitting position to start teaching your dog to "Sit." Reward them for their "obedience," and see if you can convince them to do it again.

Use small incentives to urge your puppy (or mature dog) to stay close by your side when teaching them to heel. Repeat the "Heel!" command followed by your dog's name from one side of a small apartment to the other, with your dog following by your hand. When you get to your destination, tell your dog to "Sit!" and give them their treat. Repeat the procedure until your dog understands.

Be clear about who is in charge.

Dogs use dominant language to communicate with one another in the animal kingdom. This does not imply shaming, punishing, or attempting to physically dominate your dog during obedience training. Negative reinforcement is ineffective in training puppies and adult dogs, and it can lead to nervous or destructive behavior.

Instead, when giving a command, look your dog in the eyes. Maintain eye contact until the directive is carried out. Other small psychological symbols of power include taking a daily family walk as a "pack," eating before your dog eats, maintaining a height advantage when giving commands (never kneeling to the ground level when performing obedience training), and walking with your dog behind you up a stairwell or down a narrow hallway.

Maintain your consistency.

It's all too easy to take a break from obedience training to chase and play with your puppy. However, this communicates the idea that obedience training isn't necessary. Remember that your dog is following your lead, and if you take this seriously, they will as well. Try to train your dog in 15-minute increments twice a day, and make training sessions a part of your daily routine.

Use positive reinforcement techniques.

Obedience training is a process, but it does not last indefinitely. The goal is to improve your relationship with your dog and establish clear communication between the pet and the owner. Positive reinforcement will make your dog feel like you're having fun with him, which will help him progress faster.

During training sessions, reward your dog with modest, healthy snacks for paying attention. Spend time in free play at the end of each session, such as fetch or tug-of-war. Give a special treat or a new toy when your dog achieves a goal, such as learning a new command or walking for a complete walk without pulling on the leash.

Make your house and yard dog-proof.

Obedience training, like every other new ability, has a learning curve. You don't have to sacrifice a beautifully adorned home and lush, healthy grass during the obedience training process.

In the meantime, you can do a little doggy-proofing. When your dog is alone, keep shoes, handbags, and other personal belongings out of his or her reach. Roll up rugs and remove throw pillows and blankets that could become targets for nervous energy, such as clawing and chewing, until your dog understands what you anticipate.

It may take a few weeks to teach your dog basic instructions like sit, heel, and lying down. New commands will be easier to introduce if your fluffy bestie has mastered the basics. It's worth it to persevere with obedience training, even if it takes a while; the first time your dog obeys you without prompting, you'll feel like the Dog Whisperer himself.

Training your puppy will take some time, effort, and patience. But then again, trust me when I tell you it's well worth it!

Begin with basic word training. Teach your dog to comprehend simple commands and words. You can begin crate training after this is completed. Respect and acceptance training should be implemented right away. Housebreaking takes some time, so get started as soon as possible. Once you've mastered these skills, you can begin teaching your puppy tricks. Remember not to lose patience with your puppy and to keep trying.

Finally, you are developing a relationship with your dog without even recognizing it. He will learn not just what it can and cannot do if you teach him boundaries with love and care but also that you can be trusted.

And he'll return the favor tenfold!

I wish you and your puppy the best of luck — and a lot of fun! — as you put all you've learned into practice.

Made in the USA
Middletown, DE
31 August 2022

72860136R00073